THE CLOSING NUMBERS

"Einstein said: 'Not everything that can be counted counts, and not everything that counts can be counted.' John Palumbo's magnificent book, *The Closing Numbers* is a book that counts!"

—**Myers Barnes**, MIRM, President, Myers Barnes Associates, Inc.

"Just finishing reading John Palumbo's new book titled *The Closing Numbers* with great enthusiasm, I like the simple approach on how to explain the real cost of home ownership. Wish I had read something that was so simple years ago; it sure would have made sales easier. Every sales person who wants to make more sales and increase their income should read this book to obtain John fresh approach to selling by the numbers."

—**Jerry Rouleau**, Speaker, Author & Consultant,
and Producer of BuilderRadio.com

"John Palumbo's newest book, *The Closing Numbers* is a must read for anyone in our business. It contains the essence of inserting that important dose of logic into the emotional aspect of a new home purchase. In today's market place, that logic is essential not only for purchase justification, but to ward off that dreaded buyers' remorse. Read it and Reap!"

—**Nicki Joy**, MIRM, SHMS, President, Nicki Joy and Associates, Inc.

"This is a timely solution to overcoming the 'I don't know if this is the right time to buy' objection. It makes so much sense. Truly an 'ah-ha' moment for me."

— **Gaye Burwell Orr**, MIRM, President, Coldwell Banker
Advantage New Homes

"Great communicators have the ability to reduce complex ideas to thoughts easily understood, translating into actions that produce significant results in relatively short periods of time. *The Closing Numbers* does just that in an easy to read and easy to understand format. The fear of missing the opportunities that this book opens up for you should be motivation enough to read, to understand and to use *The Closing Numbers* as your avenue to the success you have dreamed about."

—**Hal VonNessen**, MIRM, President, RESH Marketing

"In his latest book *The Closing Numbers*, John Palumbo has once again captured the true science of how to sell new homes. John has the formula to break through your limitations and make numbers your friend. Finally we have the secret to the emotional, logical and financial essence of home investment.
$E + L (U) = 2S$ will rewrite your future."

—**Bonnie Alfriend**, MIRM, FELLOW, Owner, Alfriend Sales
& Marketing Solutions and Author, *Secrets of the Superstars*

"This book is refreshing, cutting edge closing material that can be used INSTANTLY to get people to sign on the dotted line …
I will be recommending this one to all my Builder clients as a must in their sales library."

—**Melinda Brody**, MIRM, President, Melinda Brody and Company, Inc.

"Once you internalize the concept of *The Closing Numbers* you will always be able to spot that magic moment when your prospect is ready to become a bona fide buyer. John has, once again, shared a simple lesson that helps us become Master Closers."

—**Jack Gallagher**, MIRM, President, GMG Incorporated

THE +
CLO$ING =
NUMB3RS

THE +
CLO$ING =
NUMB3RS

The Art and Science of Using Hard Numbers to Sell More Homes

JOHN A. PALUMBO

Sterling
Learning
Group

www.SterlingLearningGroup.com

Foreign Rights inquiries welcome. E-mail: John@JohnPalumbo.com

For general information on our other products and services, please call (904) 448-1100.

ISBN 978-1-934381-03-8

John@JohnPalumbo.com
www.TheClosingNumbers.com
www.JohnPalumbo.com

DEDICATION

To Elwyn and Hazel Robbins

CONTENTS

Acknowledgments

Writing a book is one of the most challenging endeavors one could tackle. First it must be a labor of love. That aside, there is no way I could do it without the influence, assistance, and teamwork of some great people.

It would be impossible to mention everyone who contributed to the success of this book; however, there are some individuals who deserve special mention. That list includes Bonnie Alfriend, Tom Richey, Bob Schultz, S. Robert August, Bill Webb, Jerry Rouleau, Roger Fiehn, Meredith Oliver, Melinda Brody, Jack Gallagher, Nicki Joy, Roland Nairnsey, and Myers Barnes. I should also mention Zig Ziglar, Brian Tracy, Mark Victor Hansen, Tony Robbins, Dr. Denis Waitley, and Brendon Burchard, to name a few, for their endless inspiration and wisdom.

Special thanks to Brandon Toropov, Michelle Dorris, and Jerry Dorris for their constant attention to details, and to Yvonne Fort, Linda Rossell, Maggie Rogers, and Steve Vanderwilt, my incredibly talented team. My gratitude also goes out to Mike Friday, Gene Lambert, Lesa, Tim French, Victor Hood, Chuck D'Accardi, Ned Searcy, and Jake Aronov, for their indispensible and valued friendships and for listening to these stories way too many times.

Finaly, I'd like to thank my family, an endless source of love and support. Thanks, especially, to my mom, JoAnn, and my father, Leonard, my loving Aunt Rosalie and Uncle Tony, Heidi, and the true love of my life, my daughter, Morgan.

Introduction

You don't have to be Einstein to make my proven Closing Numbers Dialogue work for you in the new home sales industry. In fact, you don't even have to be particularly good at math.

What you do have to be, though, is ready. Ready to look at your job description a little differently. Ready to stop hiding behind excuses about "tough prospects" and "down markets." Ready to focus on some key ideas you may have overlooked in the past. Ready to take responsibility for the conversation. And last but not least, ready to review and practice a brand new way of talking about new home ownership with the people you're trying to sell to.

If you're ready ... let's get started!

CHAPTER ONE

The Lucky Guy

"Luck is a matter of preparation meeting opportunity."
—Seneca, Roman Philosopher, mid-1st century AD

A guy won half a million dollars on a pick-six lottery ticket and, still dizzy with the news, stumbled into a nearby diner. He sat down, ordered a cup of coffee, stared blankly at the winning ticket, and found himself wondering how much of the bounty he'd actually be able to keep once the taxman got his share of the winnings.

The case of the winning lottery ticket.

The waitress, a pleasant, fortyish lady with complicated fingernails and a beehive hairdo of bright red, set the guy's coffee in front of him and smiled. She noticed that he was staring philosophically at the ticket. "Get lucky with the lottery?" she asked brightly.

"Yeah," the guy replied. "But I'm trying to figure out how much I'm going to have to take off for taxes, and I really don't have much of a head for figures."

"I'm great with figures," the waitress volunteered, suddenly deeply intrigued with her new customer. "Try me."

"Well," the guy said, "somebody told me I was going to have to take off 15 percent for taxes on this money I've won, but I don't know how much that is. Can you tell me, how much would you take off for 15 percent of half a million bucks?"

Without so much as batting an eye, the waitress answered, "Honey, for 15 percent of half a million bucks, I'd take off everything."

Just like the guy in the diner, most of us tell ourselves that we "don't have much of a head for figures." In fact, the use of numbers is the weakest link in the home-sales industry.

Maybe you're wondering why you should learn about how to use hard numbers to sell more new homes. The answer has to do with emotion and logic. Numbers are an extremely powerful tool in the sales process, because they offer logical support for an emotional decision the consumer wants to make.

If you use the numbers correctly, consumers will use the numbers you give them to close the deal for themselves. A lot of salespeople are good at the first half of the equation - the emotional part - but they don't give prospective homebuyers any tools they can use to sell themselves on a deal.

Logic and Emotion

Let's face it: Buying a new home is a big decision, and when you provide the right numbers, you provide the logic necessary for the buyer to conclude the deal. If you don't provide the numbers, the result is buyer's remorse. You can set yourself up for waffling and second thoughts.

If you're interested in a sales process that results in more closings and fewer second thoughts, take a good look at this formula:

$$E + L(U) = 2S$$

Relax. It looks more complicated than it really is. (That's true of a lot of the formulas and numbers we run into on a daily basis.) Simply put, this formula means "Emotion plus Logic multiplied by true Urgency equals doubling your Sales."

Most of the salespeople I meet don't need a lot of help with the "E" in that equation - the emotion. But they fall flat when it comes to the numbers. That's a shame because we're not taking responsibility for the logical portion of the transaction. That is unprofessional in my book.

Do lawyers take responsibility for the numbers that connect to the cases they argue? Do consultants take responsibility for the numbers in the analyses they deliver? Do doctors take responsibility for the numbers that connect to the medicines they prescribe? Of course they do. And you must, too, if you want to do your job fully and professionally.

Face it: Customers expect you to know the numbers!

The people you are talking to need hard data that will make them feel good as they consider their decision after leaving you. Your goal should be to give them the ammunition they need to talk themselves into buying from you.

If you don't give them that ammunition, they'll say things like "The numbers just don't add up" or "It's just too expensive." On the other hand, if you do give them the ammunition they need, they'll say things like "That house is a great investment" or "We can't afford not to buy this place."

This book will give you the right ammunition. It will teach you a lesson that most people overlook. You will understand that there is a fundamental difference in the way that rich people and poor people think. Home ownership, in particular, reflects that difference in a powerful way.

Based on my twenty-plus years of research study in the new-home-sales industry, I can assure you that the powerful strategy I call the Closing Numbers Dialogue really works. Use it with your prospects and see for yourself!

CHAPTER TWO

Reducing The Fear Factor, Clarifying Your Intention

"It is always the simple that produces the marvelous."
—Amelia E. Barr, Author and Journalist

Let's acknowledge a simple fact: the right numbers simply don't "flow" easily for most of us in this business. So I think the best place for us to start is probably just to admit that we're not presently using figures smoothly and persuasively enough in our interactions with prospective new home buyers.

**Most of us are intimidated by numbers.
This book reduces the fear factor.**

Frankly, we're intimidated by numbers. For most of us, numbers are the missing links in our sales process. We tell ourselves that we're no good with figures or that using numbers will confuse prospective homebuyers. But you know what? Using numbers to support the new-home-sales process is a lot easier than it looks.

For those of you who hate math, I promise that this won't hurt. My goal in writing this book is to help you identify a simple set of principles that really works in your industry - the home-sales industry - and help you stick with it.

I believe the material in this book fits the bill. It is powerful, easy to apply, and highly specific to new home sales. You don't have to be a "math whiz" in order to use it.

I have had hundreds of students take the one-day course this program is based on, implement the principles and the examples you're about to see, use them the very next day, and sell a new home within 24 hours of taking my class. If you're interested in generating results like that in your own business, you might want to consider the benefits of finding a simple system for "knowing the numbers" your prospects expect you to know. (And no, shoving a preprinted form at your prospect and telling the person to fill it out does not constitute "knowing the numbers.")

Before we move on, let me share a brief note with you about the structure you will find here. You have probably noticed that this book's chapters are very short. That's because I am taking it as my responsibility not to ever make you feel that you are being "overloaded" with information. I want to make sure that the information you do get is something any "non-math major" could understand and implement.

This book was written especially for people who "don't have a head for figures" and/or "never did well in math." It was written for the lucky guy (or gal) holding a winning lottery ticket and waiting to cash it in. It was written for you.

What's your intention?

Why are you reading this book? In your own words, what's your goal?

(No, "Someone said I had to read this book" is not an acceptable answer.) Seriously, what is your objective?

Think about it. You are about to invest the most valuable asset that you have, which is time, in reading what I have to say about something I call a Closing Numbers Dialogue. Will that be worth your time? Time, after all, is money. You should never make an investment like that without knowing your objective - your payoff.

So why should you bother learning about this kind of dialogue? What do you hope to have when you get done with this book that you didn't have when you started? What do you want in return for the time you're spending?

Is your aim to sharpen your communication skills? Is it to think more quickly on your feet during discussions with prospects? Is it to build better rapport when you sit down to discuss the "hard numbers" with people? Is it simply to sell more homes?

I believe this book, if you use it correctly, will do all of those things for you, plus something additional that fundamentally supports each of those critical objectives. It will give you the tools you need to show people why it makes logical sense for them to make the substantial emotional life commitment of buying a home from you right now.

If that's what you want, you've come to the right place. I want to help you make the logical case that supports the consumer's emotional decision to buy a new home. That's what a Closing Numbers Dialogue does. It gives people good, logical reasons to act on their emotional desire to buy a home from you today. The kind of dialogue I will be sharing with you gives people logical evidence to support their emotional conviction that you're the right person to help them improve their lives through the process of selecting a new home - and that now is the right time to act.

By the way, if you don't honestly believe that you are improving other people's lives by helping them through this process of buying a home, none of what follows will work. You must honestly believe that you are adding value to their lives. You must honestly believe that what you are recommending that they do with their money today is the best possible course of action for them.

Fortunately, most salespeople I run into have the emotional part down. They are emotionally committed to what they do, they listen to their prospects, and they really do believe that what they are recommending is the right next step in their prospects' lives.

But they don't have the logical part down, the part that allows prospects to "lock in" the sale on their own after they leave your property. In most cases where there's a good match, that's exactly what home buyers really want to do - "lock in" the decision to buy a home. Whether they say so or not, people are looking for a reason to buy from you today.

As salespeople, we love to talk, but we have to learn to listen. What we do with our mouths can make us a good living. What we do with our ears can make us a fortune!

The People Business

You and I are salespeople. That means we're in the people business.

Some of those who sell homes believe that they're in the new-home business. Let me make one thing perfectly clear. You and I are not in the new-home business. We are really in the people business.

We hate to see people paying rent when they could be building up equity in a home. We have a serious moral problem with people living somewhere they don't really belong. That's the state of mind we embrace, the state of mind we radiate everywhere we go; that's the state of mind we transmit to other people. That's the business we're in.

Salespeople who don't yet know that they're in the "state of mind" business are, inevitably, poor closers. And poor closers get less fun out of life than good closers do! We have to remind ourselves constantly that we're not in business to hold hands. We're not "professional tour guides." Our business is about people. And it's about sharing a state of mind with the people we encounter, people who are making one of the most important decisions they will make in their lives: whether or not to buy a new home. So start by accepting that your goal is first and foremost to affect the other person's state of mind.

Now, I realize that that's what every marketing book, every sales book, and every book on the art of persuasion will tell you. You have to affect the other person's state of mind. But you know what? Those books usually leave out something very important: It is literally impossible for us to affect another person's state of mind if we don't first take responsibility for our own state of mind.

Your State of Mind

Contrary to popular belief, closing is not about manipulation. It's not about being slick. It's not about artful behind-the-back maneuvers. It's not about intimidation. It's really about commitment to a certain state of mind.

Using the numbers to support a certain way of looking at the world.

You can use numbers in a way that supports that state of mind in a powerful and persuasive way. And you will, if you follow my advice. But you won't be able to do this if you're not committed to taking control of your own state of mind.

The experts agree. The person who is most committed to his or her own state of mind will be the one who is most likely to affect the other person's state of mind - and sell the most new homes.

Believe it: We cannot expect to sell homes in any meaningful quantity if we have no control over our own state of mind. Our mission is therefore to cultivate a specific state of mind - and only that state of mind - and then to become so committed to it that we routinely affect the mindsets of everyone we encounter, including our prospects. Now - what, exactly, stands in the way of our doing that? To answer that question, I have to give you a little background on some research that I've done to learn what the most successful salespeople have in common. You'll find a summary of that research in the next chapters.

By the way, this book can be read alone or in combination with my book *What's Your Sales DNA?* Either approach will work perfectly well. (Visit the Web site www.MySalesDNA.com for more information about that book.) What you must understand, in the most concise words I can possibly give you, is this: You have to do some self-examination and learn to celebrate what you do well before you can accomplish anything of consequence in any field of endeavor. That's as true of new-home sales as it is of any other discipline.

If you use the principles contained in the Closing Numbers Dialogue in tandem with a consistently positive, proactive view of the world, you will be successful. If you try to use the principles that follow as though they were some kind of magic wand to wave over your prospects, while at the same time looking for reasons to feel lousy about yourself and what you do for a living, you won't be successful.

Keep working on yourself. Keep growing. Keep celebrating both your profession and your professional accomplishments. For some advice on how to do all this ... keep reading!

CHAPTER THREE

The Glass Ceiling

*"Unless you try to do something beyond what you have
already mastered, you will never grow."*
—Ronald E. Osborn, Author

Maybe you got into sales because someone told you that you
are "good with people" or because you came to believe
that the "sky is the limit." You saw the potential for unlimited
income - just by putting your people skills to work. But for
many of us, there's an invisible barrier between what we are
capable of earning and what we actually earn in the real world.
One of the names for that barrier is the "glass ceiling." You
can't see it, but it stops you from flying up where you belong.

The art of overcoming self-imposed limitations.

In the world of new-home sales, some salespeople have over-come that invisible barrier, that self-imposed set of limitations. You've met them. We've all met them. Some people call them "master closers"; others call them "sales superstars." I call them Sales Masters.

Surely you've had exposure at some point in your career to a Sales Master - to someone who achieved success at a level that left you wondering, "Wow - what is that person doing that I'm not doing?"

Unfortunately, that's the wrong question. You should be less concerned with copying the external things that the Sales Master does … and more concerned with learning how the Sales Master thinks. My research has uncovered some fascinating things about the internal self-management processes of Sales Masters. Time after time, I've found that they manage their image, emotions, and experiences in a way that delivers a certain state of belief - a powerful, confident state of mind that is rooted in a burning desire that knows no obstacle and admits no impediment. This state of mind becomes a matter of habit, something automatic that affects everyone with whom the Sales Master interacts.

Why does the Sales Master do that automatically, while other people have to make a conscious effort, or don't think that way at all? Here's the answer: the Sales Master has downloaded, and learned to operate internal mental "software" that consistently delivers that confident state of mind.

This is why asking what this person "does" to close sales is really a waste of your time. You can't get the results of a Sales Master simply by copying external activities, such as dialing the phone the same number of times, dressing in the same kinds of clothes, or saying the same things when you shake someone's hand. You have to figure out what this person does internally - how the Sales Master thinks.

Let me ask you a question. If, beginning today, you started managing your self-image, emotions and experiences - if you started thinking and experiencing your world the way top income producers do - would your commission income go up or down?

You already know the answer. Your income would go up. Why? Well, for one reason and one reason alone: Because you would be doing a better job of controlling your own state of mind. That means you would be visualizing good outcomes instead of painful ones; projecting more confidence; thinking more creatively; and delivering more effective solutions to the people you encounter during your selling day.

We are, as a group, too tentative when it comes to talking about the numbers. I'd like you to think of what follows in this book as part of the "software" for your selling career. It's something you can use to positively influence your desire, natural ability, and attitude - what I call your Sales DNA. Once you start running this "software," you will have something powerful and persuasive to say about the questions that always accompany the new-home-sales process. You'll have something to say that supports you and allows you to be more compelling in your communications with prospects - and with yourself. You will know that you're no longer one of the salespeople who simply tells customers to go "run the numbers" with a banker or real estate broker - and then "come back later and talk to us"!

If you learn to operate the Closing Numbers Dialogue "software" properly by making it a habit, I know for certain that you will be more confident in your interactions with prospective homebuyers. That confidence will make it easier for you to control your own state of mind. Yes, it takes practice and effort to control your own conscious thoughts and make good internal communication a consistent habit you can rely on. But you can learn to do it. Let me share a story with you that helped me to learn.

The Grand Machine

The story that follows is one that changed my own life for the better many years ago. I call it the parable of the Grand Machine. (You'll also find it in my book *Close and Grow Rich*.)

The great motivational author Earl Nightingale, in his best-selling, spoken-word recording *The Strangest Secret*, compared the human mind to a huge piece of equipment he once saw on a highway in the American Southwest. The machine that had captured Nightingale's attention was an earth mover, capable of moving tons of dirt from one spot to another. Imagine the biggest monster truck you've ever seen. Now multiply it by ten.

In other words, this was just a tremendous piece of machinery, lumbering purposefully, straight down the highway. Nightingale was transfixed by it. He noticed that a small man seated on top was controlling this massive piece of engineering with a tiny steering wheel.

You're behind the steering wheel.

What's the point? The human mind, according to Nightingale, is just like that earth mover. Its potential is extraordinary. Its direction depends on the tiniest twist of our mental "steering wheel." We really are in control of the vehicle - if we choose to be.

In order to take control, you have to be willing to ask yourself some critical questions over and over again: questions such as what are my intentions? What do I want? Where am I going?

At any given moment you have the power - and the responsibility - to clarify your own intention and to get very, very clear about the destination toward which you are guiding your grand machine.

Now I have a question for you. How often do you exercise that power? Do you choose the vehicle's direction? Do you choose to guide it down the highway toward a place of your choosing? Or do you take your hands off the steering wheel and allow the huge wheels to drift aimlessly? Is watching passively as the grand machine careens into the gutter - with you on it really what you want?

Of course not! So what goal on the horizon are you willing to see - to bring into your mind's eye - and steer the great machine toward? What kind of commitment do you have to course-correct, on a minute-by-minute or second-by-second basis, to keep yourself pointed toward your goal? How often are you willing to ask yourself during the course of a given day, "What is my intention? What do I want? Where am I going?"

This constant, habitual commitment to re-establishing your direction, to steering your own vehicle, must inform everything you do, including - especially including - the Closing Numbers Dialogue.

Let me be frank with you. Installing new "software" so you can update your sales DNA isn't necessarily easy. It usually takes time and effort. What's more, it takes a willingness to explore your own history. Changing your general outlook on life and your view of new-home sales in particular is a big part of that work. You must transform your outlook continuously as a matter of routine. You must move away from the habits of fault-finding and excuse-finding and toward the habits that encourage constant internal questions about your intentions, your desires, and your destination. Learning to ask yourself these questions on a regular basis really is a matter of continuous education.

The question of how to take control of all the software that determines your internal perceptions is the topic of another day and another book. The main thing I want you to bear in mind right now is that your mind really does move in the direction of its current dominant thoughts.

You can't afford to have a "bad day."

If you believe you're in a "tough market," that's what you're going to attract and experience, and that's what your prospects are going to pick up on. If you allow yourself to have that state of mind, none of what follows in this book will work.

If you're convinced that you're having a "bad day" or, even worse, a series of bad days, that's what you're going to attract and experience. That's what your prospects are going to pick up on. And none of what follows in this book will work.

In this industry, you simply cannot afford to convince yourself or anyone else that you've "gotten up on the wrong side of the bed." I've sent salespeople home for the day when I've seen them talking themselves into that kind of assumption. When there's potentially a million dollars worth of business at stake, I would much rather have a non-covered floor than have to count on someone whose guiding principle is "I'm having a bad day."

Just as dangerous are assumptions like these: "People are out to get me." "This market really stinks." Or even: "I shouldn't bother with this - I don't know enough about math to take the lead in a discussion about the numbers."

It is your responsibility. No one else's - to control your own assumptions! Some of the unproductive assumptions you experience are ideas you built for yourself. Some of them you picked up from the media. Some of them you picked up from your parents. Where they came from initially doesn't really matter. You are responsible for controlling them.

If you want to make the most of what follows in this book, you are going to have to get in the habit of challenging assumptions that disempower you. If you're ever curious about how well you're doing at challenging those assumptions, take a look at your bank account or commission check. That will reveal exactly where your Sales DNA is at any moment.

CHAPTER FOUR

The Number One Reason Why People Buy Homes

"People are never more insecure than when they become obsessed with their fears at the expense of their dreams."
—Norman Cousins, Essayist

What's the number-one reason people buy homes?

I get all kinds of answers when I pose that question during training programs. Sometimes participants tell me that people buy homes when they like the property. Others say people buy because they're going through a particular type of change in their life, such as getting married, expecting a child, or getting a divorce. Still others say it's when because the price is right, the financing is right, the home is perfect, or the landscaping is beautiful. I've even had people tell me they sold a house because the prospects smelled the aroma of fresh-baked bread the moment they walked in to tour a home. Many say their successful sales are a result of the trust and rapport they've established.

Actually, none of those are really the number-one reason people buy homes.

It's not what you think.

The number-one reason people buy homes is simpler than all of those superficial reasons I just shared with you, and at the same time it is the foundation of each and every one of them. The number-one reason people buy homes is because they perceive that other people are buying homes. In other words, people buy because they're afraid of missing out on something good that others are getting.

If you've got that much, you can pretty much guess the number-one reason people stop buying homes. That's right. They perceive that other people have *stopped* buying homes.

To put it another way, people stop buying because they're afraid of making a bad decision. They figure that the other people who aren't buying must know something they don't know about the market. Notice that fear is the governing emotion in both situations: Fear of missing out on a good thing, and fear of making a bad decision.

Here's what I want you to remember about this principle: What the fear gets connected to really is a matter of perception. Even in a supposedly "hot" buying market, people can convince themselves, or be convinced, that people "in the know" have stopped buying.

And even in a supposedly "cold" or "tough" market, people can convince themselves that the really smart folks are in there quietly taking advantage of market fluctuations - and picking up some bargains.

There are always people who are buying. It's just a question of whether or not the person you're talking to is aware of that.

Personally, I don't believe that we are ever in a "bad" economy. When everyone around me is saying "The market is collapsing," I'm saying "Now's a great time to buy ... because you can get a great value."

I believe there is something for you, the-new-home sales professional, to take advantage of in literally any market situation. It's just a question of whose perception of the realities - whose state of mind - is going to dominate in any given conversation.

In any given conversation between a prospective home buyer and a home seller, someone is going to buy something. Either the prospect is going to buy the home from you ... or you are going to buy the prospect's version of what he or she should be afraid of. It's the professional salesperson's job to create perceived value in the prospect's mind that overcomes those fears. That means that you must understand the things that are truly important to your prospects. Then use numbers to build a fire under them.

To do that, you will need to understand, and be ready to take advantage of, four foundational principles. Take a look at them now.

Principle #1: Quantify the fear of loss with "only"

We've seen that people buy homes, or stop buying homes, in response to fear, either the fear of losing out or the fear of making a bad decision.

Putting that idea of "fear" to use, we're going to conclude that the very first Closing Number we're going to look at has to do with the number one. It's about positioning the home you are selling as the only one of its kind. If we can quantify, logically, exactly how a particular home is unique and "one-of-a-kind" in an area that has some kind of emotional impact on the prospect, we can make it more likely that he or she will buy from us — to avoid losing out on that unique opportunity.

> **Find some way to position the property as unique, as "one-of-a-kind."**

For example:

This is the only home in this community that has a three-car garage.

Suddenly the property you're looking at is unlike any other. Without your having to talk about it, the prospect starts thinking about what it would feel like if someone else got that house. What's more, your credibility has gone up, because you're talking about something that's obvious, easily verifiable, and potentially of value to the prospective buyer. Who wants to miss out on a three-car garage?

That's what happens when the fear of loss is harnessed effectively. That's what Sales Masters do that most other salespeople don't do. Now compare that powerful example to this much more common, and much less effective, approach:

"This is one of fourteen homes that are currently selling for $225,000, but watch out - prices are going up on Monday."

What's unique about that? Nothing! That's more or less what everyone says. What's more, the minute prospects hear it, they are likely to think, "Baloney." (And when they drive by the property on Monday and see that prices really haven't gone up, your relationship is probably over.)

Openly threatening price increases is not an effective way to use numbers to quantify a fear of loss. This kind of doubletalk doesn't build credibility - it destroys it. You'll find advice on how to make the case for a price increase more effectively in Appendix D. For now, make a mental note that you're not ever going to claim that prices are going up on Monday (or on any specific date).

Principle #2: Reduce to the ridiculous

Again: We know that people buy homes, or stop buying homes, in response to fear. If you can use numbers to quantify, logically, exactly how small an investment really is, you can make it more likely that the prospect will buy from you. That's because the person's fear of missing out on a good deal will connect to other elements of the discussion that make emotional sense.

Make the property affordable by reframing the total cost into simpler terms in order to help your prospect see it fitting into his budget.

For instance:

The base monthly payment we're looking at is only $47 a day. Speaking personally, that's something I would want to lock in, because I know people in New York City who spend more than that on parking every day.

Look at what's happening. You're taking a monthly number that may seem scary to the prospective home buyer ... and replacing it with a daily number that puts the fear on the other side of the equation. If we don't lock in the price now, we may miss out on that $47-a-day bargain! When you say this, what are the odds that the person is going to write down and remember "$47 a day"? Pretty darned good.

But if you didn't use the parking analogy, what are the odds that the same person would only remember "$1410" (the monthly equivalent)? Very high! The person would almost certainly remember that big, scary number ... because it's higher than the $900 a month in rent the prospect is currently paying!

Which memory would you rather the person discuss or think about on the drive away from your property?

Consider the most prestigious and influential financial publication in the world: The *Wall Street Journal*. Have you ever seen that paper marketed on television? The video spots never mention the yearly price. Instead, they say something along the lines of "For only pennies a day, you can have the financial news of the world at your fingertips."

Savvy sellers and marketers know that reducing to the ridiculous activates the "buy impulse" in consumers. Numbers are powerful!

This principle applies to many of the numbers you will be dealing within all phases of the sales process. You must condition yourself to look for every opportunity to reduce to the ridiculous. This is not just a strategy - it's a mindset for selling!

Principle #3: Magnify to the magnificent

I'm going to say this once again because I want it to be tattooed on the insides of your eyelids: People buy homes, or stop buying homes, in response to fear. If you can use numbers to quantify, logically, exactly how huge the benefit of buying from you really is, you can make it more likely that prospective homeowners will buy from you. Their fear of losing out on the benefit will register in a powerful, emotional way.

Help the prospect to see that further down the road the total future benefits gained from purchasing the property exceed the long-term costs of renting.

For instance:

You know and I know that no one can predict for sure whether a piece of real estate is going to appreciate over time, or by how much. Markets go up and down. I can tell you this, though. One couple moved into this community four years ago, just a block away from here, and paid just under $200,000. It's worth a lot more than that now. When they sold, they got $360,000!

If we talked in the abstract about a "significant increase in home values over the past four years," how memorable would that be? Not very. If we use the approach above, though, is it possible the person would remember the story about the couple that earned $160,000 just for holding onto the property long enough to ride out the ups and downs of the market? You bet!

Assume that you're dealing with an apartment dweller who's

paying $1,000 a month to the landlord. What can you do to make that $1,000 per month stand out in the renters mind? Try talking about the yearly expense of renting an apartment. That's $12,000 annually! Then magnify it even further. Over the course of three years, that apartment dweller is spending nearly $40,000 for no equity! (By the way, did you notice how I used the word "nearly" to round $36,000 up to $40,000 and magnify the amount further?)

Next, suppose you are talking to someone who's considering a property that's only a short drive from his office. You might highlight the shorter commute by pointing out what it's costing your prospect to continue to drive 30 miles a day to and from work. Based on the standard IRS mileage rate of 55 cents per mile, that 150 miles a week would amount to $82.50 a week, or $4,125 a year. That's more than $12,000 over three years. And that's not even considering the cost of time spent commuting.

Principle #4: Let them connect the dots

Look at the core idea once again: People buy homes, or stop buying homes, in response to fear.

If you can use numbers to quantify, logically and persuasively, exactly how much prospective homebuyers will actually be paying for something - either in the short or long term - you can make it more likely that they will see buying from you as an opportunity to avoid paying that high cost. They will literally fear losing out on the chance to make those high payments go away. And the way to make those high payments go away is, of course, to work with you.

Let them do the math — don't answer for them.

For instance:

You: Max, you told me that you were paying $1800 a month in rent. How much do you figure that is over the course of a year?

Max: It's got to be … more than twenty thousand. Hold on. Yeah. Twenty-one thousand six hundred dollars.

You: Okay. How much is that over the course of, say, three years, if you stayed in the apartment for that long?

Max: Well - it's well over sixty-thousand dollars.

Of course, it's most effective if Max does the math in his head and says the answer himself out loud: Twenty-one thousand six hundred dollars! So that's always what you should wait for him to do. If you can get Max to say that answer out loud, it's quite possible he's going to be thinking (or saying) something like this on his way back home: "Man, twenty-one grand with no equity - that is a lot of money!"

You want to awaken the fear of losing out on a great opportunity to turn that equity-free payout into an actual investment. Therefore, ask the prospects to tell you how much they are paying in a given area over a given period of time and wait until you get an answer.

I've just given you a core secret for making the Closing Numbers Dialogue work: Don't fill in the blanks for the prospect! Pose a question that points toward an answer that supports your cause … then *wait* until you get a verbal response. In the example above, the figure "well over sixty thousand dollars" is going to be deeply memorable to Max .... because it came out of Max's mouth! (In this case, Max did the magnifying to the magnificent for you.) Now that's what I call the "Phrase that Pays!"

CHAPTER FIVE

Don't Stink Up The Joint

"The truth isn't the truth until people believe you."
—William Bernbach, Advertising Director

Can you see what I'm getting at? A truly effective salesperson in the new-home industry knows how to use the numbers to awaken a genuine fear. Also, if that fear comes in the form of a recommendation from someone who's perceived as a trusted adviser, the fear motivates people to take action - today.

False urgency smells bad.

The trick is to do that without doing what trainer Tom Richey calls *stinking up the joint* with "false urgencies." These are statements of fact that make it harder for prospects to see you as a trusted advisor. Prospects reject them (and you) out of hand because they're just too damn convenient. For instance, don't say -

- We've been really busy lately.

- There are a couple of people already looking at this home.

- I'm not going to have this home available next week.

- I have an offer coming in tonight.

When I share these examples with my seminar participants, I see a lot of people nodding their heads in sad recognition because they realize that they've said these kinds of things and have destroyed their own credibility in doing so. If you've ever said anything like this, I have a question for you. Has it worked? As in, even once?

Here's my prediction: These kinds of pronouncements have always alienated your prospects and distanced you from them. They have never brought you closer to selling a new home. Why? Because suddenly you weren't credible. People heard what you said and thought, "Baloney Sandwich!" Even if what you say happens to be true, it is presented so often by people who are lying that the truth actually turns off prospective homebuyers. So don't say anything close to what you just read.

"What if you really do have someone else looking at the property when your prospect asks whether anyone else is interested? Are you supposed to pull out a copy of the Constitution, appeal to the Fifth Amendment, and refuse to answer?" No, you can answer the person's question without stinking up the joint!

Recently, I was leasing out some office space, and a couple

of real estate agents came by to inspect the property. They were pretty excited about what they saw. About five minutes into the tour, they asked, "Do you have anyone else looking at this?"

Well, I did. But I didn't say out loud that I did. Instead, I made direct eye contact with the woman who had asked me the question, flashed my eyebrows up for a fraction of a second, and smiled broadly. She immediately smiled back and said, "You do have someone looking at this, don't you?"

I said, "Well ..." and smiled again. Then I changed the subject. They eventually leased the office space from me.

You gain stature and credibility when you let the prospect fill in the blanks. You lose all your stature and credibility when you try to build urgency in a way the prospect will perceive as blatantly false. And remember, perceptions are what matter. When the prospect's perceptions go south, you have officially begun the process of stinking up the joint.

Would you like to know another way that salespeople "stink up the joint"? By slashing prices!

Reducing prices is never - I repeat, never - the answer. At least, not from your perspective. It's possible, of course, that the management you report to might decide to lower prices at some point. But do you know what they would be obliged to do at that point? Replace the entire sales force!

Salespeople are on board to bring value to the table, not to stink up the joint!

Don't try to create false urgency. Don't reduce prices on instinct. Take control of the discussion. Take responsibility for the discussion. And start implementing the four basic principles I've just shared with you.

As a salesperson, you are paid to change perceptions and assumptions - first your own, then the prospect's. And if you truly grasp that, then you understand what your role is. That's a tall order, I know. But he who is paid well is called on to do much.

True story: The prospects walked into the model home and saw Ken walking towards them. The husband put up his hand and said, "Ken, don't waste your time, we're just looking." Ken smiled, said he understood, shook hands with each of them, and started the tour.

Ninety minutes later, the prospects bought.

As he signed the agreement, the husband said to Ken, "You know what I liked about you, Ken? You didn't push us."

They didn't know they were going to buy. Ken did. And by the way, he knew that in a supposedly "down" market!

How did he do it? He avoided stinking up the joint! He stuck to his values and used the four principles I've shared with you. He let the prospects do the talking so they filled in the blanks at all the critical points in the dialogue.

No, this book can't change "the market" for you. However, it can show you how to build up genuine perceptions of value … and then expand on those perceptions by means of a powerful, focused discussion with your prospect. That kind of discussion makes "the market" irrelevant. Once you can have that kind of discussion, you and your prospect can do anything.

CHAPTER SIX

Three Silent Precepts

"Whatever you determine to be true in the subconscious becomes true for you."
—Richard Hatch, Actor and Speaker

Here are three silent precepts - three internal monologues - that will be motivating just about every prospective homeowner you come in contact with. Because these are internal dialogues that play out at the subconscious level, you won't hear these words out loud, but you can bet your bottom dollar that your prospect is thinking them. Learn the silent precepts and learn them well. Then make sure you never, ever say anything that would confirm one of them for a prospective homebuyer.

What they're thinking when they walk in the door...

Precept number one: "Someone will lie to me at some point in this process. I don't know who it's going to be, so I'm watching all of you." (How you solve it: Say, "You should know something about us - if we can't put it in writing, we don't do it ... and we don't tell people we can do it.")

Precept number two: "Great model home - but what I see is not what I'm going to get." (How you solve it: Say, "A lot of people come in to a situation like this and see that most of our homes are under construction. They're afraid that they're not going to get what they see here in the model home. What most homeowners tell us is that they get something better." Then explain what "extras" are not on display in the model home.)

Precept number three: "I don't care how big your company is. I'm afraid you'll go out of business or leave town right after I buy." (How you solve it: Share your company's long-term business objectives. Show them where your company's going next. This is called *future pacing*.)

Those are just three of the dozens of possible internal monologues prospects are likely to bring with them when they walk in the door.

These three are among the most common, though, and you should be prepared to take the initiative and resolve them sooner, rather than later, in any relationship with a prospective homebuyer.

CHAPTER SEVEN

The Closing Curve

"If a window of opportunity appears, don't pull down the shade."

—Tom Peters, American Leadership Consultant

Sales Masters never ask for the sale before they've earned the right to. Instead, they work through a specific series of stages with the prospect. They build rapport. They ask the right questions.

They notice when they have connected with the prospect in a way that allows both of them to experience, internally, the fear that connects to one or more of the four fundamental principles I shared with you earlier. Then, at the moment of truth, a Window of Opportunity opens. The moment that window opens, and not before, Sales Masters take action.

In the world of the Sales Master, the phrase that pays is one that my grandfather shared with me: *carpe closum*. It means "seize the close." (That's a variation on the more widely circulated *carpe diem*, which is Latin for "seize the day.")

Selling effectively means seizing the close. It means noticing when and how that Window of Opportunity usually opens in your sales process. It means knowing what the optimum moment for closing typically looks like, sounds like, and feels like in your world. It means programming yourself, through continual study and habit, to identify that one critical instant in the sales process when you know you are ready to sit down with the prospective home buyer and have a good, long talk together.

When this happens between you and your prospect (and trust me, it will), the prospect will eventually reach an emotional peak as a result of your connection. Most of the time, once you've learned how to recognize that peak, you will know when it's time to talk about the numbers … and you will know when it's time to ask for the business.

To understand the Closing Curve, you don't need an advanced degree. It's just a matter of intuitively understanding a specific sequence of events that should be quite familiar to you. Take a look:

- You meet and greet the prospect(s).

- You gain information and qualify.

- You give a tour or "walk through" of the home. (That tour can be real or, in the case of a pre-sale, virtual or imaginary.)

- There's a "tingle" in the air; they like the place and you can tell that they do.

- You talk about what would have to happen for them to move in, if they chose to do so. (This should take the form of a Closing Numbers Dialogue.)

- The optimum moment for action passes.

- Then the energy in the discussion starts to fade and dissipate.

- The window of opportunity shuts, and the chance to close the deal and sell the home vanishes.

Take a close look at the diagram on the following page; return to it once daily for at least the next seven days, and study its progression with care.

Figure 1: The Closing Curve

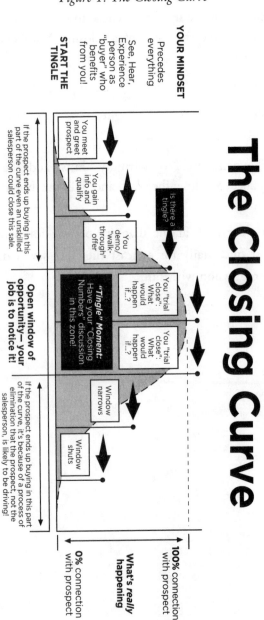

Looks familiar, doesn't it? Every time you sold a new home, this was basically what happened. Your only job is to reproduce that process. And that means noticing the process.

In my experience, success in new-home sales is simply a matter of noticing when you're at the peak of that curve. In fact, all I'm really saying with that fancy diagram is that you must learn to be a braggart like Deputy Barney Fife back on the old Andy Griffith Show. As you may recall, he used to say to the sherrif, "I'm a trained noticer, Andy."

And that's what you need to be: a trained noticer.

Watch your prospects closely, listen to them, and monitor their body language. Do this with discipline and persistence, and you will eventually develop a sense for when they have hit the very topmost point of emotion, interest, and mental buy-in. That's the "tingle" moment, when they literally can see and feel themselves living in that home.

Don't miss the peak on that bell curve! That's the point at which you will begin your Closing Numbers Dialogue. The peak of that curve is the moment when the person is totally engaged in what you're saying and thinking, the moment when you are perfectly positioned to start looking closely at the numbers with the prospect, eye to eye. This moment is where it all comes together.

You'd be amazed at how often salespeople keep chattering away about things other than closing while a prospective homebuyer has reached (or passed) the top of that peak. Don't be one of those salespeople!

Believe it: Salespeople who learn to watch the sales curve, and who use the Closing Numbers Dialogue, really do sell more new homes. Why? They "seize the close"!

Carpe closum!

In the next chapter, you'll start learning how to launch the Closing Numbers Dialogue. Before we go there, though, I want to emphasize how important it is for you to meet, greet, establish rapport and commonality, and pre-qualify the prospect before you start talking about hard numbers.

Don't underestimate the importance of the opening moments. The body language, tonality, and energy with which you greet the prospect really will affect the speed with which you move through the Closing Curve together. On the other hand, if you ignore these elements of the discussion, you may find that you don't move through the Closing Curve at all. So be sure that you...

- Make eye contact.

- Shake hands firmly.

- Find out how the person heard about you.

- Ask what the prospect(s) do for a living.

- Learn a little about the family.

- Take a look around the home (or model home) with the prospect. (Or lead an imaginary tour, if you're pre-selling. Whether it's real or imagined, your job is the same: build perceived value.)

- Get some sense of how far the prospect has gotten in the process up to this point.

You'll want to take a close look at Chapter 14, "The Art of Pre-qualifying." Pre-qualifying will help you to establish what has happened in your prospects' world, who this they have spoken to, and how much they are likely to spend.

We've reached the moment of truth. Are you ready to learn how to lead a Closing Numbers Dialogue? Good. Let's get started.

CHAPTER EIGHT

No Scripts!
(And Other Tips For Launching
The Closing Numbers Dialogue)

"There is no such thing as a worthless conversation, provided you know what to listen for. And questions are the breath of life for a conversation."
—James Nathan Miller, Journalist

'm going to share with you a *possible discussion* that incorporates a sound Closing Numbers Dialogue with a prospective home-buyer who is currently renting an apartment. There are many ways to adapt the scenario to other homebuyers, of course.

Master the art of conversation.

Let me stress the phrase *"possible dialogue."* That's what you are about to read. There is no one definitive "script" you can follow for your Closing Numbers Dialogue, and you shouldn't treat what follows as a script. All conversations with prospects are, by definition, fluid things. It's a mistake to believe that you can memorize a certain sequence of remarks and then expect prospects to respond obediently with something they are "supposed" to say.

What's more ...

Every time you go through your Closing Numbers Dialogue you will say it differently, even if you've practiced it over and over, and every time your prospect will respond in a unique way.

On each occasion the numbers you use will be different, if only because the amount of (in this case) rent the prospects are willing to accept as "reasonable," or the monthly payments they are willing to consider, is going to be different. Think of what follows as part of a fluid "teaching dialogue." You will, if you do this right, be learning how to improvise the elements of a discussion; you will not simply be memorizing as a checklist of points to cover in a certain order.

It will be vitally important for you to get verbal feedback from the prospect. It will be important, too, for you to have a general sense of the sequence of topics you will have to cover and of how to revise the order you have in mind based on what you hear. In the real world, any effective sales dialogue must flow easily, without interruption. The sample dialogue I have prepared for you here, however, unfolds in small sections, with each chapter connected to a single Key Idea, accompanied by commentary from me.

The reason for this division is simple: Each Key Idea is important, and each represents a point that must be emphasized by the Sales Master who is guiding and directing the conversation. You must understand, and be able to explain, all the Key Ideas.

If you emphasize the wrong Key Idea at the wrong time, the sale will fall apart. Make no mistake, there are dozens of places where it's very easy to make the wrong choice. By studying the Key Ideas slowly, a chapter at a time, you will get a better understanding of the choices that will be coming at you a mile a minute during an actual face-to-face encounter with a prospect.

Once you understand all the various concepts - and that's unlikely to take place unless you've read this sample dialogue at least three times and then role-played this kind of conversation with a manager or colleague - you'll be in a better position to make the choices yourself in real time.

This dialogue cannot take place before you have established the proper rapport with the prospect. If at any point you find that you're asking a question and that the prospect is responding with a blank stare or a one-syllable response, you haven't done the up-front work that's necessary to sell a home. In that case, you will want to review Chapter 7, which discusses the Closing Curve and what leads up to the all-important peak of that curve.

W.A.R.

The dialogue that follows is a declaration of war on the whole concept of rent. Like any good sales technique, its goal is to compel action by maximizing the perceived pleasure of action or the perceived pain of inaction.

Highlight pain and pleasure.

Fortunately, it's fairly easy to call attention to the pain associated with continuing to pay rent. It's equally easy to help people experience the pleasure they can anticipate from earning equity in a private home that they own themselves. Amazingly, though, the vast majority of the new-home-sales professionals I run into have never learned to exploit the pain-and-pleasure principle effectively. In our industry, that's close to professional malpractice!

If you take the time to become intimately familiar with the "War on Rent" discussion that follows, and to practice it, I can promise you that you will not be one of those salespeople who are guilty of malpractice. You'll be at W.A.R. Do you know what that means? It means you're a Warrior Against Rent. It means you are at war against the pernicious, dangerous habit of thinking like a renter instead of a homeowner!

I believe rent is sapping the very financial life-blood of far too many American families. I firmly believe that if there is even one family in this country who is renting when home ownership is a realistic financial option, that's one family too many. Do you believe that?

Never forget: You need to be the leader of the conversation; you need to declare open war on the whole concept of rent.

I hate rent ... and you know what? You should hate it, too! Are you really a Warrior Against Rent? If you are, you take rent personally, because paying rent keeps tenants from building up equity. It keeps them from ever benefiting from inflation. In fact, apartment-dwellers have the biggest reason to curse that perpetual thief. Rent keeps millions from starting the noble mission of taking control of their own financial future.

As far as I'm concerned, rent is a trick designed to keep land-lords fat and happy, sipping piña coladas down in the tropics … using other people's hard-earned cash. That's how I feel about rent, and it's not an act. It's genuine. In fact, here's what I always tell people about rent every chance I get. Paying rent if you don't have to is not just foolish - it's morally deficient. That's the principle I always come back to when I'm talking to apartment-dwellers: paying rent is basically immoral.

If someone who's currently renting an apartment looks at a home I'm representing and then tells me, "John, I have to think about it," I feel obligated to set them straight. I view doing less than that as a moral lapse, something close to a breach of professional responsibility on my part.

If you believe as I do - if you have a firm conviction that you can improve the financial and lifestyle realities of the families you encounter by helping them grasp the real-world numbers that prove, definitively, the superiority of owning over renting - you have an obligation to help people take control of their financial destinies. I urge you to make that your declaration. Join me in becoming a Warrior Against Rent (W.A.R.). Take up your sword (the pen) and prepare to do battle!

Figure 2: No Rent

KEY IDEA: Wait for the Right Moment.

There will be a Right Moment, a moment when you know for certain that you have bonded with the other person, a moment when you are confident at a very deep level that the time has come to move forward and look at the numbers. At that moment, and not before, you will want to begin focusing on the Closing Numbers Dialogue that will help you close the deal with this prospective homeowner.

You are the only one who can possibly say when that moment has arrived. Not the prospect. Not your sales manager the morning after the meeting. Not me. If any author of any book tries to tell you otherwise by suggesting that someone other than you can identify when you've actually bonded with someone, I suggest that you demand your money back.

I realize that this may be a frustrating thing for you to read. You no doubt would rather have me tell you that you should introduce the Closing Numbers Dialogue into your conversation with a prospect at a specific point. But, unfortunately, there's no magic formula. I can't tell you to do it twenty-two minutes into the meeting, immediately after the prospect asks you a direct question that shows interest in the home, or when you and the prospect share a laugh. The problem is that each of those "guidelines" will collapse the instant you try to use it as a real benchmark for conversations in the real world.

All I can tell you is that the Right Moment will become more and more recognizable to you after you've sold homes for a while. If you don't know what I'm talking about right now, you can rest assured that the Right Moment definitely won't take place until …

- after you've established some point of commonality with the prospect, perhaps during the period of time when you are showing off the property.

- after there's a meaningful dialogue that incorporates real "back and forth."

- after you have some sense of the person's income, debt load, and ideal monthly payment.

- and after you've noticed the "tingle" in the air arising from the real possibility of a match.

I've been in situations where the Right Moment came along after what seemed to be a dozen dead ends and many hours of discussion. I've also been in situations where the Right Moment popped up literally minutes after I'd begun a conversation with a prospect. When it comes along, though, you will want to initiate a conversation that sounds something like this:

YOU: Tell me a little bit about the place you're staying in right now. How big is it?

PROSPECT: It's a little bit smaller than this place. Only two bedrooms, and not as large as this home. But it does have two baths, just like this one. Of course, this looks a lot nicer from the outside, and it's in a lot better neighborhood than my apartment.

Notice that you've received confirmation, just from this much of the conversation, that it's a good idea to follow your instinct and make your entry into the "hard numbers" portion of the discussion.

Why? Because the response you got from the prospect was a fairly lengthy one. In fact, the prospect's response was longer than your question! Always a good sign.

If you'd asked that same question and gotten an answer like, "It's smaller," followed by stony silence and an unwillingness to meet your gaze, you'd know for certain that it was not a good idea to proceed with the Closing Numbers Dialogue that follows in subsequent chapters.*

KEY IDEA: Dialogue, not monologue.

So far, we're assuming that you've asked a question about the prospect's current lodgings. Where should you go from there? Well, if it was me, and I didn't already have the information, I might pursue the discussion by asking about the amount of rent the person is presently paying.

Remember, we're basing everything on the assumption that

---

* By the way, I'm not saying that all prospects are likely to talk a blue streak once you've bonded with them. There will definitely be some people who give you terse responses, and nevertheless want to hear more from you. Natural introverts can bond with you, too. The question is: how do you tell these folks from the people who aren't ready to have a serious discussion with you about home ownership? Check the eye contact. Do they return your gaze, or are they wary about looking you in the eye? Check the body language. Do they seem relaxed and open, or are their arms crossed? The former signal is a green light, and the latter is a red one. Is the person's curved index finger "locked" in front of his or her pursed lips while you're speaking? If so, the person with whom you're interacting is almost certainly feeling defensive, anxious, and uncertain about you. Is the person supporting the conversation with "ideomotion" - that is, silent nods and other participatory nonverbal messages - or staring at you blankly, without moving much as you talk? If you're getting only passive, negative signals, you are not yet regarded as a trusted advisor. You have not yet earned the right to proceed to your Closing Numbers Dialogue.

this person is willing to share information. If you ask for pertinent information like what the monthly rental bill is, and you get no meaningful information in return, you're simply not ready to move forward!

But let's assume that there really is some good chemistry up front with this person and that the conversation proceeds as follows:

YOU: I had a feeling you'd like the neighborhood here. A lot of people tell me it feels very family-friendly.

PROSPECT: Yeah, I could see how they'd say that.

YOU: You have two kids, right?

PROSPECT: That's right, a boy who's nine and a girl who's seven.

YOU: I can remember when mine were that age. It was a lot easier than dealing with teenagers, I'll tell you.

PROSPECT: Yeah, I bet.

YOU: Tom, how much does a two-bedroom, two-bath place like yours go for?

What I want you to notice here is that I'm not simply jumping into the request for financial information. I'm making it part of a larger social exchange with the prospect and highlighting a common experience I share with him, namely parenthood. Look how very different that exchange is from an exchange where the prospect says, "Yeah, this is a lot better neighborhood than where we're renting now," and I instantly jump in with, "How much a month do you pay in rent?"

I can't emphasize this point enough: Commonality and rapport make everything that follows in this dialogue possible. And it really must be a dialogue, not a monologue masquerading as a dialogue.

In contrast, here's what a monologue masquerading as a dialogue sounds like:

YOU: Got kids?

PROSPECT: Uh-huh.

YOU: How many?

PROSPECT: Three.

YOU: Still in an apartment?

PROSPECT: Uh, yeah.

YOU: How many bedrooms?

PROSPECT: Two.

YOU: Sounds crowded.

PROSPECT: Sometimes, I guess. It's okay.

YOU: How big is the place?

PROSPECT: I don't know ... what, do you mean like square footage?

YOU: Either that or the number of rooms.

PROSPECT: Oh. Two bedrooms. Kitchenette. Living room

YOU: Uh-huh.

PROSPECT: That's about it.

YOU: And how much are you paying for that?

PROSPECT: Way too much.

No matter how much seeming back-and-forth takes place in such a discussion, it's not really a dialogue. You haven't gotten the other person to open up in any meaningful way. As long as there's an emotional barrier between you and the prospect, this can only be a monologue masquerading as a dialogue.

No Lockdowns!

KEY IDEA: "Would it help ...?"

Suppose, however, that you've established rapport and commonality. You know there's some good back-and-forth in the discussion and you have asked, directly, how much this person is paying in rent every month. If you've established yourself as the trusted advisor you claim to be, you should encounter no resistance to that request. As a result, this is what the exchange should sound like:

YOU: Tom, how much does a two-bedroom, two-bath place like yours go for?

PROSPECT: It's $900 a month.

Okay. What happens next?

Remember, your goal is to get the prospect to feel the pain

of the current situation and to anticipate the pleasure of home ownership. At this stage, you might be tempted to do that by asking something like, "Isn't that a lot of money to be throwing away every month, considering that you're not building up any equity in the property you're living in?" That's called stinking up the joint!

The problem with that kind of question is that it instantly destroys the good will and credibility you've built up with Tom so far. How do you feel when somebody asks you a question that can accommodate one and only one "right" answer? Consider the last time a telemarketer called you up and asked, "Would you be willing to talk to me if I showed you a way you could save two million dollars in the next four minutes?" Technically, you're supposed to only be able to answer "yes" to that. In actual fact, though, that kind of question makes most intelligent people feel they have no alternative but to answer "no." In short, this is a "lockdown" question, and it's a hallmark of a way of selling that no longer moves homes (or much of anything else) in quantity.

That kind of "lockdown" question convinces people that we are out to corner them, manipulate them, and force-feed decisions to them. Nobody likes to be force-fed. Once you've convinced them that that's what you're after, you will find that it's very difficult to get them to feel pain about the rent they're paying, or feel pleasure about the equity they could be building up. The only thing they will feel is wariness, because they'll have raised their defenses against you for asking such an obviously manipulative question.

Do you remember the precepts we discussed earlier in this book, the strong preconceptions that virtually all prospective homebuyers have entering into this process? If so, you remember that one of them is a certainty that someone, at some point in the home-buying process, is going to lie to or mislead the prospective homebuyer. You definitely don't want to give the prospect any evidence of that. So that means you definitely don't want to sound like an overanxious telemarketer. Instead, you want to sound like a professional.

Here's one example of a professional continuation of this conversation:

YOU: Tom, how much does a two-bedroom, two-bath place like yours go for?

PROSPECT: It's $900 a month.

YOU: And how does that compare to the monthly payment range that you're considering right now?

PROSPECT: Well, it's a good deal lower, obviously.

YOU: How do you mean, lower?

PROSPECT: Well, if you figure a monthly mortgage payment, of, I don't know, $1100 ... it's just going to be a higher figure than the $900 we're paying in rent right now.

YOU: You know what? You'd be surprised how often that's not the case. Would it help if we took just a minute to break the numbers down, so we could see whether or not it makes sense to own or rent?

Here, you're not trying to box anyone into anything. You're offering to help. Big difference!

Assuming that the prospect says yes you're ready to move forward with the Closing Numbers material. If the prospect says no, you're either not dealing with a qualified buyer or you didn't do the right emotional preparation up front. We'll bank on the fact that you're still talking with someone who is interested. Now watch how the dialogue gets serious.

> YOU: *Would it help if we took just a minute to break the numbers down, so we could see whether or not it makes sense to own or rent?*

> PROSPECT: *Sure.*

> YOU: *Let's have a seat. I'm going to make some notes and share them with you, all right?*

I do recommend that you pursue the remainder of this conversation while you're seated with the prospect. It's also a good idea to use some kind of "permission statement," like the one I've shown you above, before you start jotting down figures on your legal pad. Be sure your handwriting is legible; if it's generally tough to read, make a point of writing larger than usual.

From this point forward, the notations you make on that legal pad to show your prospect will be indicated in this typeface.

> YOU: *Let's say you were to stay in the apartment you're in right now. You say it's costing you $900 a month, right?*

> PROSPECT: *That's right.*

> **(You write:)**
> **$900**

> YOU: *Okay. I'm going to come back to that number a little later, because I want to show you the true monthly cost of renting versus the true monthly cost of owning.*

The phrase "true monthly cost" is important. Make sure you lay that groundwork at this point; you'll be revisiting this idea later on in the presentation.

You continue:

YOU: Now, let's start looking at the monthly investment of home ownership versus the cost to rent an apartment. Your home is $180,000. Let's look at that number.

PROSPECT: Okay.

(You write:)

$900   **$180,000**

Again: Interaction matters! If the prospect isn't interacting with you, as I've said above, there's a problem. Take a break and try to get the back-and-forth going before you proceed any further.

KEY IDEA: Control the vocabulary.

You're now going to plug in a number that's connected to the initial investment the prospect is anticipating making on the new home. If you've already figured out what that number is, your job is fairly easy. You just write down the number and confirm it with the prospect. If your previous discussions didn't get to this point, the dialogue is going to sound something like this:

YOU: Now, let's start looking at the monthly investment of home ownership versus the cost to rent an apartment. Your home is $180,000. Let's look at that number.

PROSPECT: Okay.

(You write:)
$900   *$180,000*

YOU: *What kind of initial investment - in other words,
down payment - were you anticipating making up front? Five
thousand, ten thousand, fifteen thousand, twenty thousand
…?*

PROSPECT: *Let's say fifteen thousand.*

YOU: *Okay, fifteen thousand.*

(You write:)
$900   *$180,000*
                               -$15,000
                               $165,000

Please notice three important things.

First, you're educating the prospect in a new vocabulary, sub-stituting the phrase "initial investment" for the old phrase "down payment." From here on out, having made this substitution, you're only going to be talking about the "initial investment." You're never going to talk about the "down payment." You'll be doing the same thing with "monthly investment" a little later on; that's going to replace the scary-sounding "monthly payment." Your Closing Numbers Dialogue must employ your vocabulary for such terms, not the prospect's!

Second, you're giving the prospect a lot of options to choose from when it comes to specifying that initial investment. This is called "bracketing," and it's an extremely important technique to master.

Lastly, you're waiting for the prospect to say a number out

loud. You're making sure the other person fills in the blanks.

Now, when you ask this question about the initial invest-ment, you must ask it with complete and unshakable confi-dence, and you must make direct eye contact with the prospect as you do so. Your demeanor at this stage must be that of a doctor asking about symptoms, not a salesperson in search of a commission!

Competence equals confidence!

At this point, it helps to have a calculator handy so you can figure out the interest rates on what a monthly base payment or investment might be for this prospect. (Notice that I called it a "base" payment or investment, not a "mortgage" payment. That's an important distinction, as you'll see in a moment.)

Note: If for some reason you find you're not comfortable figuring out interest rates, you'll probably want to work out a table that features the most common monthly breakdowns during these discussions.

You: Now let's assume a six and a half percent interest rate on a thirty-year loan of $165,000. (You punch the numbers into the calculator.) That's going to be a base monthly investment of $1043.

(You write:)

$900 $180,000

                                  -$15,000

                                  $165,000

                                  = base mo. investment

                                  $1043 (6.5%, 30 yrs)

You will want to highlight the base monthly numbers now.

You: Now, here's where it starts to get interesting. (You highlight the numbers :)

$900	*$180,000*
	-$15,000
	$165,000
	= base mo. investment.
	$1043 (6.5%, 30 yrs)

YOU: Obviously, the $900 is the smaller number, right?

PROSPECT: Yep.

YOU: It's about to look even smaller. Watch. That's just the monthly base. We left out some things on the "house" side. And I wanted to show you the true cost of ownership, so we're going to list everything.

You're about to make it crystal clear to the prospective homeowner that you're completely committed to taking full account of all the possible expenses he or she will face.

Building Credibility

*"Death and taxes and childbirth! There's never
any convenient time for any of them."*
—Margaret Mitchell, Author

KEY IDEA: Add dollars to the house side.

The dialogue should continue along the following lines:

*YOU: Of course, with home ownership comes additional
responsibility. There are going to be property taxes to pay every
month on your home. My experience on a property like this is that
it's going to be about $1800 a year, or about $150 per month.*

(You write:)

$900 $180,000
                             -$15,000
                             $165,000
                             = *base mo. investment*
                             $1043 (6.5%, 30 yrs)
                             +$150 *property tax*
                             = $1193

You just referenced your experience in the marketplace (which is almost certainly greater than that of the prospect) as a reason for adding dollars to the homeownership side, an action that would seem to undercut your "side" of the discussion. Assuming that you've actually established commonality and rapport with the prospect, this simple act will build credibility in a more significant way than almost anything you can do. It also reinforces that you've been around the block a few times, and that you know how things tend to add up in different municipalities. Most importantly, though, it allows you establish your own integrity in this process. You're adding expenses to the "house" column.

You must do something like this early on in your Closing Numbers presentation. This property tax "estimate" is probably the best place to do it.

KEY IDEA: Add more dollars.

Having incorporated the property taxes, you're going to continue adding dollars to the "home ownership" side of the equation. When you do so, it's going to sound like this:

YOU: Now, in addition, there are going to be insurance costs. I might estimate that at seventy-five, but let's use an estimate of one hundred, just to be safe.

PROSPECT: Okay.

(You write :)

$900

$180,000
-$15,000
$165,000
= base mo. investment
$1043 (6.5%, 30 yrs)
+$150 property tax
= $1193
+ 100 insurance
= $1293

Obviously, the same basic principle is in play. You'll use it once again when you estimate the maintenance costs:

YOU: Then there are maintenance costs - you know, repair and upkeep. Let's call that $50 a month. Fair?

PROSPECT: Sure.

YOU: On second thought, let's up it a little and say $75.

(You write:)

$900

$180,000

-$15,000

$165,000

= *base mo. investment*

$1043 *(6.5%, 30 yrs)*

+$150 *property tax*

= $1193

+ 100 *insurance*

= $1293

+ $75 maintenance

= $1368

That's not one, not two, but three instances of additional dollars you've volunteered to throw into the "home ownership" column. If you've done your job this far into the discussion, you've built up a significant level of credibility.

You're about to capture the attention of even the most jaded rent-payer.

KEY IDEA: Tax advantage.

This next part represents a critical turning point in the dialogue because it's the first place you're going to justifiably subtract dollars from one of the totals. You must, of course, execute what follows with complete self-assurance. Here's what it should sound like:

YOU: Now, once you own the home, you get a tax break on the interest, Tom. Remember, I told you we were going to get a look at the true cost of renting versus the true cost of owning. Here's where the homeowner gets the tax break that the landlord would normally get if you were renting. If you're paying $1043 a month as your monthly investment, let's say that, on a yearly basis, approximately $10,500 of that will be interest. I'm going to assume a tax rate of 28% in your case, based on what you told me earlier. So that would mean a monthly tax savings of about ... $245.

(Confirm all this on your calculator for the prospect.)

In addition, you're going to be able to deduct 28%* of the total property taxes you pay, which is going to come out to about a $504 tax break every year, and that, divided by twelve, is about ...

(Confirm all this on your calculator for your prospect)

... $42 per month. So let's get both of those in. $245 plus $42 gives us a total tax advantage of about $287 every month. This is where the government helps you own the home!

---

* Disclaimer: Many renters find themselves unable to itemize deductions. This occurs when the standard deduction ($10,900 for married couples filing jointly in 2008) exceeds the allowed itemized deductions. The renter may not get any benefit from itemized deductions even though they have considerable itemized expenses.

(You write:)

$900

$180,000

-$15,000

$165,000

= *base mo. investment*

$1043 (6.5%, 30 yrs)

+$150 property tax

= $1193

+ 100 insurance

= $1293

+ $75 maintenance

= $1368

- $287 income tax advantage

= $1081.

Wow! Suddenly the prospect is interested. This is beginning to make sense.

KEY IDEA: Appreciation.

You're about to talk about the financial concept of appreciation in a way that won't make the prospect's head hurt. Here's how:

YOU: Of course, there's another advantage to owning over renting, and that's appreciation. You can never be sure that an investment is going to increase in value over time, of course, but real estate has a pretty good record over the long haul compared to just about any other investment. Now, if you were going to make an estimate of how the value of your home would change on a yearly basis, what would you estimate?

PROSPECT: I don't know … how about twelve percent?

YOU: I agree with you - that would be a realistic estimate. But I'm a conservative person. What do you say we reduce it a little bit? (Stop talking.)

PROSPECT: Okay. How about nine percent a year?

YOU: That's not a bad estimate, and there are a lot of properties we could use to back it up. But can we be even more conservative? Some salespeople use crazy numbers to make their case, and I want to make absolutely sure we're putting in something you're comfortable with.

PROSPECT: Six percent?

YOU: Even lower.

PROSPECT: You've got me … say three percent? Or four?

YOU: Okay. We probably couldn't get much more conservative than that. Let's use three percent. Is that OK with you?

Tom has just given you "permission" to use a 3 percent appreciation figure. And that's exactly what you want … even though it looks, for the entire world, like you've been bargaining in the wrong direction.

Three percent was where you wanted to end up all along. There's an important reason to use 3 percent as your base figure here, above and beyond the fact that fixing a low number for the estimate you're about to make builds credibility with the prospect. I'll share the reason for using that 3 percent appreciation rate, rather than any other number, in a later chapter.

For now, just remember that your goal is to get the 3 percent figure to come out of the prospect's mouth, not yours. Notice that you're doing something most salespeople don't do: You're reducing expectations about how much the property is going to appreciate over time. To do that, you've taken Tom's own numbers and gotten him to reduce them!

KEY IDEA: Take away more dollars.

Here's how you'll actually use that 3 percent figure in the discussion. Watch what happens to the true cost of home ownership. (You can rest assured that that's the figure the prospect will be watching.)

> YOU: *On your home of $180,000, if we plug in your figure of an appreciation rate of 3 percent, which means it's going to gain about $5,400 in the first year. (Confirm this on the calculator for the prospect.) When you break that down to a monthly figure, it comes out to about $450 a month. To get to the true cost of ownership figure, we're going to have to back that out, too.*

(You write:)

$900

$180,000
-$15,000
$165,000
= *base mo. investment*
$1043 (6.5%, 30 yrs)
+$150 property tax
= $1193
+ 100 insurance
= $1293
+ $75 maintenance
= $1368
- $287 income tax advantage
= $1081
- $450 appreciation
= $631 true monthly investment!

YOU: *So when you figure everything in on the home ownership side, the true cost of ownership is how much, Tom?*

PROSPECT: *Wow ... that's less than six hundred bucks.*

YOU: *Hold on. We're not done yet.*

You're certainly not done yet. To put it bluntly, you're about to blow the prospect's mind.

KEY IDEA: Tax advantage to renting?

You're about to pose a question that ninety-nine out of a hundred people will answer with some variation on the word "No."

That's exactly the response you want ... because you know that the best answer is really "Yes!"

YOU: Now, this brings me to a question. Is there a tax advantage to renting?

PROSPECT: Um ... no, I don't think so.

YOU: That's where I have to disagree with you, Tom. There is a tax advantage to renting ...

PROSPECT: There is?

YOU: ... but let me be specific ... there is a tax advantage to renting ... if you're the LANDLORD! Let me illustrate this for you. Do you remember that $287 you took as a tax deduction on the interest and property tax payments?

PROSPECT: Yeah.

YOU: We're going to move it over to the renting side ... and this time, we're going to add, rather than subtract. The fact that the landlord gets it means you don't!

(You write:)

$900	*$180,000*
+$287 income tax advantage	*-$15,000*
= $1187	*$165,000*
	= base mo. investment
	$1043 (6.5%, 30 yrs)
	+$150 property tax
	= $1193
	+ 100 insurance
	= $1293
	+ $75 maintenance
	= $1368
	- $287 income tax advantage
	= $1081
	- $450 appreciation
	= $ 631 true monthly investment!

The message is clear: Rent is considerably more expensive than your prospect ever imagined.

If you've done everything correctly up to this point, you will have all of the momentum of the conversation on your side. It will be easy for you to continue to dramatically illustrate the pain of paying rent. And that's just what you're going to do.

Example of Tax Advantage

A married couple makes $180,000. They have two children. They rent a three bedroom home. They pay their own health insurance ($1,000 a month premium and $200 a month in co-pays, prescription and over-the-counter drugs, mileage to the doctor/

hospital, eye care, etc). They pay state and local income or sales taxes of $2,500 a year. They contribute $100 a week to charities, churches, etc. (less than 3% of their income). Lastly, they have combined unreimbursed mileage (over 50 cents a mile) and other employee expenses of $6,500. For tax purposes, they would have approximately $10,800 in allowed itemized deductions. Due to various limitations on itemized deductions, the $28,600 in above expenditures gives them zero tax benefit. The $10,900 standard deduction is used because it exceeds the allowed itemized deductions.

These types of renters are prime candidates to receive the full tax benefit (in the above example - 28%) of owning a home and deducting the mortgage interest and real estate taxes. If the above taxpayers bought a house and incurred $11,000 in mortgage interest and $1,800 real estate taxes, they would save almost $300 a month in taxes.

Taxpayers in these types of situations should consult a tax adviser to be sure itemized deductions are being fully utilized.

CHAPTER TEN

What It Really Costs

"The rich aren't like us; they pay less taxes."
—Peter De Vries, Editor and Satirist

KEY IDEA: Landlord's appreciation.

---

on't stop now. You're headed for the finish line. Make it perfectly clear how much paying rent is really costing the prospect.

YOU: You can see that the landlord gets some great tax breaks from the government just by virtue of the fact that you're renting from him. But now back to you, Tom. As a renter, do you think there's any appreciation?

PROSPECT: Well, no ... I don't think so ...

YOU: *Actually, the answer is not what you'd think. There is probably appreciation occurring. The problem is, once again, it's going to the landlord. Those apartments are more than likely going up in value, just like this home should for you as the owner. So instead of the $450 monthly advantage you would get from home ownership ... the landlord gets an advantage, because his apartments are going up in value. You see what I mean?*

PROSPECT: *Yeah.*

YOU: *So for simplicity's sake, let's just use the same number to illustrate the appreciation. Now it goes to the landlord. Take a look.*

(You write:)

$900	*$180,000*
+$287 income tax advantage	*-$15,000*
= $1187	*$165,000*
+$450 appreciation	*= base mo. investment*
= $1,637 total cost to rent!	*$1043 (6.5%, 30 yrs)*
	+$150 property tax
	= $1193
	+ 100 insurance
	= $1293
	+ $75 maintenance
	= $1368
	- $287 income tax advantage
	= $1081
	- $450 appreciation
	= $ 631 true monthly investment!

YOU: You see where I'm shining a spotlight? What's your true cost of renting, Tom?

PROSPECT: Wow. Looks like over sixteen hundred bucks!

Suddenly, what once looked like a "cheaper" alternative - $900 in monthly rental costs - is seen for what it really is: a wasteful, indefensible lifestyle choice!

KEY IDEA: Some "closing" points.

At this stage, you can expect any number of reactions from the prospective buyer. Depending on the personality of the individual, and depending on how good a job you've done on all the early-stage connection and the tour of the home or model home, you may get a solemn nod of agreement, or you may get a little pushback. (As in "Very nice use of the numbers, John.") However, if you have gone over the Closing Numbers Dialogue properly, you will be engaged in a conversation about what should happen next, and that's definitely where you want to be!

You will, of course, need to tailor your response to the feedback you get once you share this "Rent on Steroids" demonstration with your prospective buyer. Consider incorporating some or all of the following bullet points, which have been immensely helpful to me over the years in closing the deal after sharing this Closing Numbers material with prospects. The biggest lesson in these "closing" points, as you will see, has to do with the fundamental difference in the thinking of rich people and poor people, as you will see. This is, of course, the point you have been leading up to all the time.

YOU: Let me ask you something, Tom, do you think that, at night, when your landlord goes home to have dinner with his wife, he says to her, "Honey, I have a warm feeling inside - because I'm providing shelter for a bunch of needy people." No! He's in this to make money, and he's out to make it as easy as possible for you to continue renting from him. I think you can see why, given the numbers we've just gone over.

When you go home tonight, and you realize that your landlord is getting rich off you and hundreds of people like you, you'll realize why people like you decide to go ahead and purchase a home and invest in their future now. Because every day that goes by costs you money.

Tom, the statistics say that you will stay in that apartment for something like three more years if you walk away from here today. That means how many dollars a year going down the drain every year - with no equity and no appreciation?

(If Tom gives you no answer after a prolonged pause, magnify to the magnificent with the attention-getting answer: "Almost $20,000 a year!" That's his true cost of renting - $1,637 - times twelve months - or $19,644. Walk Tom through the figures! Then conclude with: "I just can't see your choosing to throw that kind of money away.")

You wonder why landlords say things like "You won't have to worry about the roof leaking!" or "You won't have to worry about mowing the grass!" Of course the landlord wants to make it easy for you to live in that apartment.

(Maybe Tom says something like: "Look, nice job with the numbers. But I still can rent for $900, and I just can't swing ten-fifty a month. Can't do it! ")

Well, I'm going to say this once - and I'd say it whether you considered going to someone else or bought from me - the difference between the $1,637 it costs you to rent that apartment, which really is your true cost to rent, versus the $631, which is the true ownership investment, is the real reason

THE RICH GET RICHER
AND THE POOR GET
POORER.

Tom, let me be frank with you. Understanding this concept is what makes the difference between those two groups.

(It's up to Tom now. Let him choose which group he really wants to belong to. If he doesn't close himself at this point, you may choose to continue with...)

Again - the statistics say, Tom, that if you walk away now, you will keep renting for another three years or so. But you may be different. You may be able to ... (slight pause for emphasis) make the decision now ... (another slight pause) and move forward. Some people do, some people don't. It's up to you.

Now, here's the key to making any of these "closing points" - and indeed the entire system - work. We have to do two kinds of work up front.

The first kind of "work" I'm talking about has to do with your ability to visualize success before it happens. Before you even shake hands with your prospects, you have to envision them happy that they're not paying rent anymore. That's what you have to process internally before you meet your prospects. They've been renting for years, and finally they're in a home they own. You see, hear, and experience your prospects being really, really jazzed about that before you even get face to face!

Then, when you're face to face and they really do get jazzed about this idea, you can literally sense the little tingle that goes through their bodies. And after you've had a few years of experience, you can help turn that little tingle into a big tingle by communicating your own passion in a way that they can connect with.

CHAPTER ELEVEN

Plant A Seed

"All personal breakthroughs begin with a change in beliefs."
—Anthony Robbins, Author and Speaker

There's a second kind of "up-front work" that's necessary for this Closing Numbers Dialogue to deliver good results for you. And that has to do with what I call "planting a seed."

You may recall, earlier in the book I insisted on your engaging in a dialogue with your prospects to determine a workable (low) figure to represent estimated annual appreciation on the property they are considering purchasing. If you go back and review the dialogue, you'll see that what I shared with you followed this sequence:

- You pointed out that no one actually knows what the value of real estate will do over time.

- You asked the prospective homebuyer to provide an estimated annual rate of appreciation for this property. (Very important: You did not offer that number yourself.)

- The prospective homebuyer offered a number. (In our example, he suggested 12 percent a year.)

- You then engaged in some back-and-forth, getting lower and lower numbers from the prospect, who finally offered 3 percent as a conservative number that you could both live with as a "rough guess."

This conversational sequence, which is essential to the Closing Numbers Dialogue, is only possible if you do the work up front by "planting the seed."

As you were reading the Closing Numbers Dialogue through for the first time, perhaps you thought to yourself, "That's not very realistic. If I ask a prospect to tell me what the rate of appreciation on a property is going to be, he's just going to stare at me and say he has no idea."

You're right. If you don't plant the seed beforehand, that's exactly what's going to happen.

You must do the right work up front. Long before you even begin the Closing Numbers Dialogue, you must discuss the subject of appreciation with your prospects! When you ask for an estimate of appreciation, you must provide the benchmarks they need to give you an answer. That means you must have a very good idea what that number is going to be.

Well before starting the Closing Numbers Dialogue, you must

say something like this to the prospect, in a way that registers:

> *Over the past seven years, property values in this township*
> *have increased by almost 15 percent a year.*

Notice that you've picked a time-frame - seven years - that allows you to point to a significant, verifiable increase!

That one detail, consciously chosen, should give you an idea of the control you really have over this process. It really doesn't matter if the last year has seen a drop in overall home values - you can choose a window in which there was an upward trend: three years, say, or five years, or any other time-span that works for you. You could also have chosen a different region - the whole county, say, rather than a single township. The goal is to chose a statistic intelligently, connect it meaningfully to your prospect's world, and then weave it into your early conversation with your prospect in a memorable way.

This is planting the seed! It's an extremely important skill, especially in a down market. Of course, some people will be skeptical about the likelihood that real estate will appreciate in value. What can you do? Take the lead from stockbrokers who face a very similar - and in fact a far more daunting - challenge. Find the right time window and exploit it! Early on in a conversation, professional stockbrokers will talk about how a given stock has performed over a carefully chosen time frame. They're planting the seed!

The test for whether you have planted the seed properly is simple. During your Closing Numbers Dialogue, when you finally ask prospects to give you an estimate for the rate at which they feel the property will appreciate one of two things can happen.

Either they will be able to give you a number, in which case you will know that you've done your job, or they won't be able to give you that number, in which case you will know that you haven't.

I'm not saying that the number has to leap off your prospect's tongue the instant you ask the question. There may be (and often is) a pause in the conversation while the prospect thinks back on what you said earlier about appreciation. You may even need to give a subtle reminder about what happened over the last seven years in this township. But at some point your prospect will come up with a number. Once that happens, you can start the process of encouraging him or her to whittle it down.

If you plant the seed ahead of time, you will have no problem getting a number from your prospect. And you can be sure your prospect will not object as you make the estimate more and more "conservative" - until the 3 percent figure you're after emerges. I promised you an explanation for the necessity of getting your prospect to arrive at 3 percent as the estimate for appreciation on the property. Here it is.

There's a deeply pragmatic reason to insist on the "3 percent solution" I've outlined in chapter nine ... and never to accept an appreciation estimate that is higher than 3 percent. To put it bluntly, 3 percent is the only consistently safe number you can use.

Let's say you were to accept the prospect's suggestion of 9 percent as the estimate on the annual appreciation on the property. What would happen? Your whole presentation would fall apart.

Compare the "3 percent solution" I gave you in earlier in the book with this "9 percent disaster":

YOU: On a home worth $180,000, if we plug in an appreciation rate of 9 PERCENT, which means it's going to gain about $16,200 in the first year. (You confirm this on the calculator for the prospect.) When you break that down to a monthly figure, it comes out to about $1350 a month. To get to the true cost of ownership figure, we're going to have to back that out, too.

(You write:)

$900

$180,000

-$15,000

$165,000

= *base mo. investment*

$1043 (6.5%, 30 yrs)

+$150 property tax

= *$1193*

+ *100 insurance*

= *$1293*

+ *$75 maintenance*

= *$1368*

- *$287 income tax advantage*

- $1350 appreciation

=NEGATIVE $269!

Watch out! Since you plugged in the first number the prospect gave you - that optimistic 9 percent annual appreciation rate - you now have to explain why it suddenly looks as though the person is going to be paid three hundred dollars a month to live in your property. You can expect a wave of rapport-destroying ridicule at your expense if you are ever unlucky enough to land yourself in this spot. So don't.

Remember: You're using numbers to dramatize the effects of ignoring the benefits of property ownership. That's all you'll ever be doing, and all you'll ever claim to be doing. If you don't play it safe, though, by sticking with the reliably credible "3 percent solution" you've seen used in the sample Closing Numbers Dialogue I've given you, you'll end up dramatizing something else … namely, your own clumsiness with numbers or, even worse, your lack of personal credibility!

It's also important to remember that because we have no idea what property values will do in the future, you can only use facts and historical data to help carve a vision of the future. Never promise a future value or guarantee appreciation. Your job is to allow the prospective buyer to draw their own conclusions.

CHAPTER TWELVE

Why It Works

"A good plan is like a road map; it shows the final destination and usually the best way to get there."
—H. Stanley Judd, Author

If you use it correctly, the Closing Numbers Dialogue you've just seen works.

Believe it. The version I've given you really, truly works when it comes to selling homes to people who are currently throwing away their money by renting. With very minor variations, the same basic ideas can (and have) been used to sell to people who are "empty nesters," to people who are moving out of their parent's place for the first time, to people who are considering purchasing a condominium, and to any number of other prospective buyers.

You can do anything with the model that you want to do … if you implement it as I've suggested here.

The dialogue won't work if you try to use it as a security blanket. You can't quote it verbatim to someone without having built up trust and credibility. You can't try to use it to instantly turn the person from a skeptical "No, thanks, just looking" contact to a "Hey, where do I sign" contact. But the model definitely does work if you use it as a road map, as a guide to the most important destinations along the way in the journey that we call a "really great conversation" with a prospect. And those are the conversations that close sales.

Think of what you've just seen as the lay of the land, the most notable features of a specific terrain you want to travel on a regular basis. That terrain is called "The Land of Conversations that Lead to Closing." Personally, I've used the dialogue with what I must honestly call extraordinary success. I haven't used it as a verbatim script, of course. By now it should be obvious that I hope you won't try to use it that way, either. But I have used it as a broad outline for specific talking points with people who were interested in buying new homes. I've used intelligent variations of the Closing Numbers Dialogue you just read to sell literally thousands of properties over the years. The people I've trained, both on sales teams and during face-to-face seminars, have sold even more homes than I have using these same talking points. If you connect the dots and use the same principles to raise the same issues, you'll probably sell a lot of new homes, too.

You may be wondering why it works. I'll give you two reasons.

We've already covered reason number one: The Closing Numbers Dialogue works because it capitalizes effectively on the prospect's fear. Remember, the number-one reason people buy homes is because they perceive that other people are buying homes.

They're afraid of ... what?

You've got it. They're afraid of missing out on an opportunity that they may not have again. After you've given a good Closing Numbers presentation, they're also afraid of subsidizing the landlord's lifestyle at the expense of their own. The dialogue kindles those two fears, strengthens them, offers evidence for them, and makes them more compelling and powerful.

As for reason number two - well, you just saw it in action. A few sentences ago I asked you to complete a question of mine. Remember? Here's what you read: "They're afraid of ... what?"

Because you're reading this book, you probably didn't say anything out loud in response to that question, and you almost certainly kept reading so you could get the answer. If this were a face-to-face discussion between the two of us, though, and if I had built up sufficient rapport with you to win the right to pose that kind of direct question, something very interesting would have happened.

You would have answered the question for yourself, or you might have asked me for help in answering it. You would have had to, because I certainly wouldn't have said anything after posing it!

There would have been some interplay, some connection, some back-and-forth between the two of us. And that's reason number two that the Closing Numbers Dialogue really works. It's a tool for interaction, a tool for getting the other person to say something within the structure of a larger dialogue whose destination is familiar to you, but not to the prospect.

I think the most beautiful thing about the Closing Numbers

Dialogue is its flexibility. You can adapt it to virtually any situation. You can use the same basic conversational landmarks to sell a $270,000 home as you would to sell a $2.7 million dollar home. Just move the decimal point over.

The most dangerous thing about the Closing Numbers Dialogue is probably its eloquence. I'll bet you can almost hear it playing out in your head as you read the words, and it probably sounds pretty good. In fact, because of its eloquence, you may come to think that you can simply cover all the points and close the deal. You can't. You still have to build rapport. You still have to gather information. You still have to understand the Closing Curve. You still have to know when you're at the top of that curve.

This outline I just shared with you can't make someone buy who doesn't want to buy. No discussion outline can do that. There is simply no skill called "forcing a $270,000 decision down someone's throat." If there were, you wouldn't have to concern yourself with things like finding out what you have in common with prospective buyers and learning what their unique "hot buttons" are.

Since this is the real world, you do have to concern yourself with those things. As long as you bear that in mind, and treat the Closing Numbers Dialogue as a tool, rather than a crutch, you'll do fine.

CHAPTER THIRTEEN

Play By The Numbers

*"The difference between a mountain and a molehill
is your perspective."*
—Al Neuharth, Founder of USA Today

Later in this book, you'll find some important guidelines on pre-qualifying, on the art of what I call "downselling by the numbers," and on how to raise the sensitive issue of future price increases. After that, you'll find a glossary that will give you authoritative definitions for some of the most common terms you and your prospective homebuyers will encounter during the buying process.

Before you move on to any of that, though, I want to close by reminding you to make absolutely sure that you are always, but always, playing by the numbers. Knowing the numbers and using them effectively can literally double your commissions. Abusing the numbers can get you in a great deal of trouble.

You probably don't need this reminder, but I'm going to pass it along anyway. Commit to the highest standard of personal and professional ethics. Make every human effort live up to that standard each and every day, and make it a habit to talk about your ethical standards with prospective homebuyers.

In particular, I want to remind you of your obligation to …

- Make no guarantees that a home will appreciate in value.

- Make no representations about the value of a home that you can't support with objective, external data.

- Make only truthful representations about the value of a given property.

- Treat all parties honestly.

- Protect and promote the interests of the buyers you work with.

- When estimating something outside of your own direct experience, make it clear that your estimates are only estimates.

That's what true Sales Masters do. Those are the rules I play by. They should be the rules you play by, too. Now let me tell you a little bit about what I believe.

I believe that real estate, as a category, will always outpace every other investment in the long term, no matter what happens in the short term. I believe that people always have, and always will, buy homes during both "good times" and "bad times," and that the great salespeople are the ones who make those sales happen. I believe that the best salespeople - the category of salespeople I call Sales Masters - bring value to the table for everyone they do business with, and that they are proud to do so in a transparent way.

If you are willing to use the tools I've given you to become that kind of salesperson - the Sales Master whose every move is above board and whose ambition is consistently to deliver value - then you are the person for whom I wrote this book. Play hard, play strong, and always play by the numbers.

I'm big on summarizing information, condensing it down to its absolute essence. I find it easier to implement information when it's been boiled down in this way. So, here comes this whole book in a nutshell. Ready?

Numbers = logic.
Logic = sale
No logic ... no sale!

Another Summary

Here is a summary of all the Key Ideas for the Closing Numbers Dialogue you read in this book.

Dialogue, not monologue.

"Would it help ...?"

Have a seat.

Control the vocabulary.

Add dollars to the house side.

Add more dollars.

Tax advantage. Appreciation.

Take away more dollars. Tax advantage to renting?
Landlord's appreciation.

"Closing" points.

(The rich get richer, and the poor get poorer!)

Go forth and prosper!

CHAPTER FOURTEEN

The Art Of Pre-qualifying

Here's how I like to pre-qualify prospective home buyers. I look the person right in the eye and ask, "Have you talked to a banker, an attorney, a mortgage loan officer, or any other professional to find out what price range you'd be qualified for?"

(Up to this point, I've been gesturing toward the prospect. When I say the words "any other professional," I point all five fingers of both hands back toward me, while maintaining eye contact with the prospect. This is a subliminal piece of "programming" that builds rapport and puts me in the same category as the professionals I've mentioned.)

If I get a no answer, I simply ask, "Would you like to know?" If the person is genuinely in the market, I always get an affirmative reply. With the confident air of a doctor making an important diagnosis, I maintain that all-important eye contact and ask prospects to "ballpark " some figures for me: their household income (including the income of the spouse), total debt, and how much they are planning to put down as a down payment. I then work up an estimate that I explain is likely to be roughly what they will hear from a banker or mortgage broker. Before we part company, I recommend a banker or mortgage broker for them to reach out to. Of course, I call the financial person immediately and let him or her know what I've learned about the prospects.

In my experience, salespeople are just too easily frightened when it comes to asking people about their finances. If you're going to do a good job in this industry, you've simply got to be willing to ask people directly - and purposefully - about their money situation. If you do so as a professional who's eager to find a way to help them make a big choice correctly, and if the prospects truly are interested in buying a home, you won't find any resistance.

What's the alternative? If you avoid the subject entirely, you risk showing your prospects the wrong home. If you point your prospects toward a banker or mortgage broker who is not expecting the call and knows nothing whatsoever about the prospects, how professional is that? It's a lousy alternative ... but that, all too often, is exactly what happens in our industry.

CHAPTER
FIFTEEN

The Art Of Downselling
By The Numbers

What do you do when you have to sell a home that's not as desirable as some of the others in the same development or neighborhood? Suppose the property is backed up against a power line, and its view is less than ideal. I like to "downsell by the numbers" in that kind of situation.

Suppose the homeowner tours the property and says something like, "John, I do like the floor layout, and the southern exposure is what I'm looking for, but the view out the back window isn't great."

You know what I say?

"Tom, that's actually the whole reason I brought you here. You're saving $30,000 on this home, and it seemed to me like it matched up with the price range you and I were kicking around. Let me share with you what Bill, the gentleman who lives next door, decided when he saw that view. He and I were talking about it recently. When he bought the property, he said, 'I think what I'm going to do is take the $30,000 I'm saving and decorate the house with it!' His wife was ecstatic. She's just going to throw up a big curtain against that back wall. For Bill, the view was the reason to get in."

The reason to take this approach is simple: You win both ways.

The buyer who wants a bargain will listen to your logic. You're painting a picture for him of how he can get into the community without going out of his price bracket. The fear of losing that opportunity is going to start to feel very real to him, because you're effectively planting the seed of that opportunity and "watering" it with that great story about how Bill "used" the $30,000 he saved.

You win on the other side, as well. The prospective buyer who doesn't see this price break as a great advantage is making a buying statement … and upselling himself! Show him something a little pricier.

CHAPTER SIXTEEN

How To Discuss Price Increases

I've already warned you against stinking up the joint with false urgencies that the prospective homebuyer will consider implausible at best. Of all the possible false urgencies home-sales professionals try to foist on prospective buyers - and there are quite a few - the one that most consistently rings hollow is the one where we tell buyers something like the following:

You know, our prices are going up next week.

Virtually every single time you say something like this, the other person thinks, "Baloney." And, as I mentioned earlier in the book, the relationship is effectively dead, because you've lost all credibility. You say the prices are going up next week, and the prospects are absolutely certain that one week from now they will be the same. Whether or not that's true, it's what the prospect perceives to be true, and that is what matters.

Fortunately, there's a better way of raising precisely the same issue, without losing any of your hard-won credibility. The trick here is to avoid saying directly that prices are going up at any specific date or time. Instead, get the prospective home buyer to be the one who says, out loud, that a price increase can come at any time, with no warning whatsoever. Here's how it works.

Let's assume I'm talking to a prospect with whom I've built up a good deal of rapport, and who's looking at, and seriously considering, a specific property. We've talked about the benefits of the particular location; we've identified something that makes this property "one of a kind" for this unique buyer. We've figured out together that this is the only property that has A, B, and C.

If I'm in that situation, and I want to land the point that a price increase is a very real possibility on this specific property, I will say something like this:

> *Mr. and Mrs. Smith, one of the reasons I want you to think about going ahead and tying this up today is that I literally never know when our prices are going to change. I can't tell you that they're going up at any particular day or time - I never know that. But I can tell you that we have the best pricing that we will ever have on this property right now. And just so you know, here's what happens when our prices go up. It happens when I'm sitting in the office and I check my e-mail. There's an attachment, which I open and print.*

Then a piece of paper comes through the printer ...

At this point, I mime the action of picking up the sheet of paper by its top two corners. I'm now "holding" an invisible sheet of paper carefully, as though not to smudge it.

… and I go to look at it … and guess what it says on that piece of paper?

Here I carefully turn around the (invisible) piece of paper so the prospect can "read" it. Then I stop talking and wait for the prospective homebuyer to answer the question. Inevitably, the person says, "The price just went up?"

That's when I nod knowingly and look at the person directly and expectantly, as though I were asking, "So what did you want to do about this?"

I've closed a lot of deals this way. Try it. This really is a winning formula for raising the "price increase" issue without making a "false urgency" claim (like "prices are going up on Monday") that the other person will very likely reject outright. It's much stronger when the other person tells me that the price of the home he wants is in danger of going up!

Glossary

1031 exchange - a real estate transaction "involving the sale of one property with the tax on the capital gain deferred because of the qualified purchase of another like-kind property in exchange." (Source: Investor Glossary.)

203 (b) - FHA program that provides mortgage insurance to protect lenders from default. It is used to finance the purchase of new or existing one- to four-family housing; characterized by low down payment, flexible qualifying guidelines, limited fees, and a limit on maximum loan amount.

203 (k) This FHA mortgage insurance program enables homebuyers to finance both the purchase of a house and the cost of its rehabilitation through a single mortgage loan.

Acceleration Clause - provision allowing the lender to ask for full payment at once, if loan installments are not paid when due.

Accrued Interest - interest that is due, on a bond for example, but that hasn't yet been paid.

Actual Cash Value - an amount equal to the replacement value of damaged property minus depreciation.

Adjustable Rate Mortgage (ARM) - a mortgage loan subject to changes in interest rates; when rates change, ARM monthly payments increase or decrease at intervals determined by the lender. The change in monthly payment amount, however, is usually subject to a Cap.

Adjustment Period - the time between interest rate adjustment dates for an ARM. They are usually the initial period between the time the ARM is originated and the first interest rate change date, and subsequent adjustment periods between each interest rate change after the first interest rate change.

Adverse action - (1) refusal to grant credit in the amount or under the terms requested, or (2) termination of an account, or (3) refusal to increase the amount of an existing credit line when the applicant requested it in accordance with the creditor's procedures, or (4) an unfavorable change in terms that affects only some of the debtors.

Advice - the credit union's written acknowledgment to its members of a debit or credit transaction affecting that member's account.

Amenity - a feature of the home or property that serves as a benefit to the buyer but that is not necessary to its use; may be natural (like location, woods, water) or man-made (like a swimming pool or garden).

Amortization - a term used to describe the process of paying off a loan over a predetermined period of time at a specific interest rate. The amortization of a loan includes payment of interest and a portion of the outstanding principal balance during each payment cycle.

Amortization Schedule - a table showing the amounts of principal and interest due at regular intervals and the unpaid mortgage balance after each payment is made.

Amount Financed - the amount of credit provided to or on behalf of the borrower, calculated under the Truth in Lending Act. This is the principal minus certain loan charges that the Truth in Lending Act defines as finance charges.

Annual Percentage Rate (APR) - calculated by using a standard formula, the APR shows the cost of a loan expressed as a yearly interest rate. It includes the interest, points, mortgage insurance, and other fees associated with the loan.

Application - the first step in the official loan approval process. This form is used to record important information about the potential borrower necessary to the underwriting process.

Application Fee - the fee that a mortgage lender charges to apply for a mortgage to cover processing costs.

Appraisal - a document that gives an estimate of a property's fair market value. An appraisal is generally required by a lender before loan approval to ensure that the mortgage loan amount is not more than the value of the property.

Appraisal Fee - charge for estimating the value of collateral being offered as security.

Appraiser - a qualified individual who uses his or her experience and knowledge to prepare the appraisal estimate.

Appreciation - an increase in the market value of a home due to changing market conditions and/or home improvements.

Arbitration - a process where disputes are settled by referring them to an impartial third party (arbitrator) chosen by the disputing parties who agree in advance to abide by the decision of the arbitrator. There is a hearing where both parties have an opportunity to be heard, after which the arbitrator issues the decision.

Assessor - a government official who is responsible for determining the value of a property for the purpose of taxation.

Asset - anything owned by an individual, a business, or a credit union which has commercial or exchange value.

Assumable Mortgage - a mortgage that can be transferred from a seller to a buyer. Once the loan is assumed by the buyer, the seller is no longer responsible for repaying it. There may be a fee and/or a credit package involved in the transfer of an assumable mortgage.

Assumption - a homebuyer's agreement to take on the primary liability for paying an existing mortgage from a home seller.

Audit - an official investigation to verify that all assets, liabilities, income and expenses of a financial institution are correctly stated. The audit of an institution's operation also serves to inhibit fraud and errors, and determines the accuracy of accounting and bookkeeping procedures.

Average Daily Balance - a method used to determine interest on a loan balance. Purchases and advances for the month are added to the outstanding balance, and then credits are subtracted. The result is divided by the number of days in the month.

Bait-and-switch schemes - the lender may promise one type of loan or interest rate, but switch you to a different one. Sometimes a higher (and unaffordable) interest rate doesn't kick in until months after you have begun to pay on your loan.

Balloon Mortgage - a mortgage that typically offers low rates for an initial period of time (usually 5, 7, or 10) years; after that time period elapses, a "balloon" (lump sum payment) is due at the end of the term. Balloon mortgages frequently contain a provision to refinance when the balloon payment is due.

Balloon Payment - any payment that is more than twice the amount of any other regularly scheduled equal payment.

Bankrupt - a debtor who is judged legally insolvent and whose remaining property is administered for distribution among his creditors.

Bankruptcy - a federal law whereby a person's assets are turned over to a trustee and used to pay off outstanding debts. This usually occurs when someone owes more than they have the ability to repay.

Basis Point - a unit of measure for the change in interest rates that is equal to .01 percent (for example- 100 basis points equal 1%).

Bear Market - a period when the stock market in general declines.

Bearer - the person actually holding a legal instrument, such as a check, payable to "bearer" or endorsed in blank.

Beneficiary - a person who is entitled to the balance in an account upon the death of the owner (trustee) of the account.

Beta - a measurement of a stock's performance calculated from past price patterns indicating how much a stock price can be expected to move in relation to a change in the market as a whole.

Blanket Mortgage - a mortgage covering at least two pieces of real estate as security for the same mortgage.

Bond - a) An interest-bearing certificate of debt, usually issued by a government or corporation, by which the issuer obligates itself to pay the principal amount at a specified time and to pay interest periodically. b) A legal contract by which an insurance company agrees to pay, within stated limits, for financial loss caused by the default or dishonest acts of a third party.

Bond Rating - a judgment about the ability of a bond issuer to fulfill its obligation to pay interest and repay the principal when it is due.

Borrower - a person who has been approved to receive a loan and is then obligated to repay it and any additional fees according to the loan terms.

Broker - a member of a stock exchange firm or an exchange member who handles orders to buy and sell securities and commodities for a commission.

Budget - a detailed record of all income earned and spent during a specific period of time.

Bylaws - the rules adopted by the shareholders and board of directors to define the field of membership, set the par value of shares and give the general method by which corporate functions are to be operated.

Cap - a limit, such as that placed on an adjustable rate mortgage, on how much a monthly payment or interest rate can increase or decrease.

Capacity - one's ability to make mortgage payments on time. This depends on income and income stability, assets and reserves, and the amount of income each month that is available after paying for housing costs, debts and other obligations.

Capital gain (and loss) - the difference between the sale price and the purchase price of an investment.

Cash Reserves - a cash amount sometimes required to be held in reserve in addition to the down payment and closing costs. The amount is determined by the lender.

Certificate of Deposit (CD) - an instrument that is issued by the credit union in the name of the member stating that a certain sum of money is on deposit and that the member agrees to keep this money at the credit union for a certain period of time. CDs vary widely in amount and term, and the rate of interest depends on both of these factors.

Certificate of Title - a document provided by a qualified source (such as a title company) that shows the property legally belongs to the current owner. Before the title is transferred at closing, it should be clear and free of all liens or other claims.

Certified Check - a personal or business check for which payment is guaranteed by the drawee bank. Proof of the guarantee is shown when the bank stamps the word "certified" on the face of the check.

Charge Off - to treat as a loss.

Check Clearing - the process of sending checks through the nation's banking system for delivery to drawee financial institutions for final payment against the makers' checking accounts.

Check Hold - practice used by most financial institutions to ensure checks on deposit will, in fact, be paid by the drawee bank. It was developed to protect consumers and financial institutions from fraud and bounced checks.

Check Truncation - the practice of storing checks at the credit union rather than returning them to the member. When a check first enters the check-clearing process, the information on the check is captured and transmitted by computers to the drawee bank. The check itself is not sent through the nation's check clearing system. All account transaction information is included on a member's monthly statement. Members may request copies of specific checks.

Closed-End Credit - credit contracts that specify the time period over which the loan or sales contract will be repaid, the total amount due, and the number of payments and due dates on which they fall.

Closing (Closing Date) - also known as the settlement date, this is the time at which the property is formally sold and transferred from the seller to the buyer. At this time the borrower takes on the loan obligation, pays all closing costs, and receives title from the seller.

Closing Agent - a person that coordinates closing-related activities, such as recording the closing documents and disbursing funds.

Closing Costs - customary costs above and beyond the sale price of the property that must be paid to cover the transfer of ownership at closing. These costs generally vary by geographic location and are typically detailed to the borrower after submission of a loan application. They include expenses such as points, taxes, title insurance, mortgage insurance, commissions, and fees.

Collateral - property, which is pledged as security for a debt. In the case of a mortgage, the collateral would be the land, the house, and other buildings and improvements.

Collateralized Loan - loan in which member owns collateral free and clear (i.e. car, boat, recreational vehicle).

Comaker - a person, other than the borrower, who signs a note in order to give additional protection to the creditor granting the loan, because of the uncertain credit quality of the borrower.

Commission - an amount, usually a percentage of the property sales price that is collected by a real estate professional as a fee for negotiating the transaction.

Commitment Letter - a letter from the lender that states the amount of the mortgage, the number of years to repay the mortgage (the term), the interest rate, the loan origination fee, the annual percentage rate and the monthly charges.

Compound Interest - interest added to the principal and itself begins to earn interest.

Concession - something yielded or conceded in negotiating a transaction.

Condominium - a form of ownership in which individuals purchase and own a unit of housing in a multi-unit complex. The owner also shares financial responsibility for common areas.

Consolidation Loan - combining several debts into one loan, usually to reduce the annual percentage rate or the dollar amount of payments made each month, thereby extending them over a longer period of time.

Consumer Loan Act (CLA) - a law that authorizes higher interest rates so as to ensure credit availability to borrowers with higher-than-average credit risks that might otherwise be unable to obtain loans.

Consumer Protection Act (CPA) - a law that prohibits unfair and deceptive acts or practices in trade or commerce.

Conventional Loan - a private sector loan that is not guaranteed or insured by the U.S. government. Federally backed loans include Federal Housing Administration (FHA), Veterans Administration (VA) and U.S. Department of Agriculture Rural Development loans (formerly Farmers Home Administration or "FMHA" loans).

Cooperative (Co-op) - residents purchase stock in a cooperative corporation that owns a structure. Each stockholder is then entitled to live in a specific unit of the structure and is responsible for paying a portion of the loan.

Co-signer - a person who guarantees the payment of a loan for another person.

Counter-Offer - an offer made in return by the person who rejects the previous offer.

Credit Bureau Score - a number representing the possibility a borrower may default. It is based upon credit history and is used to determine ability to qualify for a mortgage loan.

Credit history - history of an individual's debt payment. Lenders use this information to gauge a potential borrower's ability to repay a loan.

Credit Rating - the estimate of the amount of credit that can be extended to a borrower without undue risk based on the borrower's past credit experience.

Credit Report - a record that lists all past and present debts and the timeliness of their repayment. It documents an individual's credit history. Can also contain public information such as bankruptcies, court judgments, and tax liens.

Credit Score - a computer-generated number that summarizes an individual's credit profile and predicts the likelihood that a borrower will repay future obligations.

Credit Scoring System - a quantitative, statistical evaluation method used to establish a credit applicant's creditworthiness.

Credit Union - a cooperative financial institution that provides consumer financial services for members of a specified group as defined by its charter (CUs may be federally or state chartered).

Creditworthiness - an evaluation of a consumer's ability and willingness to repay a debt.

Debt - a sum of money owed from one person or institution to another person or institution.

Debt-To-Income Ratio - the relationship between the consumer's monthly debt payments and monthly income, expressed as a ratio. Lenders will often set a maximum debt-to-income ratio and usually do not make loans to consumers whose ratios exceed the lender's standard. With the FHA, the-monthly mortgage payment should be no more than 29% of monthly gross income (before taxes) and the mortgage payment combined with non-housing debts should not exceed 41% of income.

Declining Balance - the decreasing amount owed on a debt as monthly payments are made.

Deed - a formal, written agreement transferring title of a real estate property from one person to another.

Deed of Trust or Mortgage - a legal document in which the borrower conveys the title to a third party (trustee) to hold as security for the lender. When the loan is paid in full the trustee re-conveys the deed to the borrower. If the borrower defaults on the loan the trustee will sell the property and pay the lender the mortgage debt.

Deed-In-Lieu - to avoid foreclosure ("in lieu" of foreclosure), a deed is given to the lender to fulfill the obligation to repay the debt. This process doesn't allow the borrower to remain in the house but helps avoid the costs, time, and effort associated with foreclosure.

Default - failure to perform a legal obligation. A default includes failure to pay on a financial obligation, but may also be a failure to perform some action or service that is non-monetary.

Default Rate - the interest rate the creditor will charge once the borrower defaults on the loan. This rate is always higher than the contract interest rate.

Delinquency - failure of a borrower to make timely mortgage payments under a loan agreement.

Demand Deposit - checking account funds that are subject to withdrawal at anytime on demand by a member's written demand (usually a check).

Deposit - the amount of money one puts down on a house to hold it.

Depreciation - a decline in the value of a house due to changing market conditions, decline of a neighborhood, or lack of upkeep on a home.

Direct Deposit Service - a process that credits a member's bank account directly for a payment due the member without the use of a check, e.g. (a monthly Social Security payment)

Disclosure Statement - an itemized list of all charges giving total cost of credit.

Discount Point - normally paid at closing and generally calculated to be equivalent to 1% of the total loan amount. Discount points are paid to reduce the interest rate on a loan.

Disposable Income - take-home pay, or net pay.

Diversification - the method of balancing risk by investing in a variety of securities.

Dividend - a share of earnings distributed to shareholders of a credit union.

Dollar-Cost Averaging - a program of investing a set amount on a regular schedule regardless of the price of the shares at the time.

Dormant Account - a member account that has had no deposit or withdrawal activity for a certain period of time.

Down payment - the portion of a home's purchase price that is paid in cash and is not part of the mortgage loan.

Draft - a signed, written order, which is addressed by the maker to the drawee, to pay a sum of money to a third person, the payee.

DRIP - stands for direct investing plan, dividend reinvestment plan, or reinvestment plan. A DRIP is a program under which a company automatically reinvests a shareholder's cash dividends in additional shares of stock.

Earnest Money - money put down by a potential buyer to show that he or she is serious about purchasing the home. It becomes part of the down payment if the offer is accepted, is returned if the offer is rejected, or is forfeited if the buyer pulls out of the deal.

Energy Efficient Mortgage (EEM) - an FHA program that helps homebuyers save money on utility bills by enabling them to finance the cost of adding energy efficiency features to a new or existing home as part of the home purchase

Equity - an owner's financial interest in a property, calculated by subtracting the amount still owed on the mortgage loan(s) from the fair market value of the property.

Escrow Account - a separate account into which the lender puts a portion of each monthly mortgage payment. An escrow account provides the funds needed for such expenses as property taxes, homeowners insurance, mortgage insurance, etc.

Fair Housing Act - a law that prohibits discrimination in all facets of the homebuying process on the basis of race, color, national origin, religion, sex, familial status, or disability.

Fair market value - the hypothetical price that a willing buyer and seller will agree upon when they are acting freely, carefully, and with complete knowledge of the situation.

Fannie Mae - Federal National Mortgage Association (FNMA) a federally-chartered enterprise owned by private stockholders that purchases residential mortgages and converts them into securities for sale to investors. By purchasing mortgages, Fannie Mae supplies funds that lenders may loan to potential homebuyers.

Federal Housing Administration (FHA) - established in 1934 to advance homeownership opportunities for all Americans. It assists homebuyers by providing mortgage insurance to lenders to cover most losses that may occur when a borrower defaults. This encourages lenders to make loans to borrowers who might not qualify for conventional mortgages.

Fixed-rate Mortgage - a mortgage with payments that remain the same throughout the life of the loan because the interest rate and other terms are fixed and do not change.

Flood Insurance - insurance that protects homeowners against losses from a flood. If a home is located in a flood plain, the lender will require flood insurance before approving a loan.

Foreclosure - a legal process in which mortgaged property is sold to pay the loan of the defaulting borrower.

Freddie Mac: Federal Home Loan Mortgage Corporation (FHLM) - a federally-chartered corporation that purchases residential mortgages, securitizes them, and sells them to investors. This provides lenders with funds for new homebuyers.

Ginnie Mae: Government National Mortgage Association (GNMA) - a government-owned corporation overseen by the U.S. Department of Housing and Urban Development, Ginnie Mae pools FHA-insured and VA-guaranteed loans to back securities for private investment. As With Fannie Mae and Freddie Mac, the investment income provides funding that may then be lent to eligible borrowers by lenders.

Good Faith Estimate - an estimate of all closing fees including pre-paid and escrow items, as well as lender charges. It must be given to the borrower within three days after submission of a loan application.

Homebuyer Education Learning Program (HELP) - an educational program from the FHA that counsels people about the homebuying process. HELP covers topics like budgeting, finding a home, getting a loan, and home maintenance. In most cases, completion of the program may entitle the homebuyer to a reduced initial FHA mortgage insurance premium-from 2.25% to 1.75% of the home purchase price.

Home Inspection - an examination of the structure and mechanical systems to determine a home's safety; makes the potential homebuyer aware of any repairs that may be needed.

Home Warranty - offers protection for mechanical systems and attached appliances against unexpected repairs not covered by homeowner's insurance; coverage extends over a specific time period and does not cover the home's structure.

Homeowner's Insurance - an insurance policy that combines protection against damage to a dwelling and its contents with protection against claims of negligence, or) inappropriate action that result in someone's injury, or) property damage.

Housing Counseling Agency - provides counseling and assistance to individuals on a variety of issues, including loan default, fair housing, and homebuying.

HUD: the U.S. Department of Housing and Urban Development - established in 1965, HUD works to create a decent home and suitable living environment for all Americans. It does this by addressing housing needs, improving and developing American communities, and enforcing fair-housing laws.

HUD1 Statement - also known as the "settlement sheet," it itemizes all closing costs; must be given to the borrower at or before closing.

Heating, Ventilation and Air Conditioning (HVAC) - a home's heating and cooling system.

Index - a measurement used by lenders to determine changes to the interest rate charged on an adjustable rate mortgage.

Inflation - occurs when the number of dollars in circulation exceeds the amount of goods and services available for purchase. Inflation results in a decrease in the dollar's value.

Insurance - protection against a specific loss over a period of time that is secured by the payment of a regularly scheduled premium.

Interest - a fee charged for the use of money.

Interest Rate - the amount of interest charged on a monthly loan payment; usually expressed as a percentage.

Judgment - a legal decision; when requiring debt repayment, a judgment may include a property lien that secures the creditor's claim by providing a collateral source.

Lease Purchase - assists low-to-moderate-income homebuyers in purchasing a home by allowing them to lease a home with an option to buy. The rent payment is made up of the monthly rental payment, plus an additional amount that is credited to an account for use as a down payment.

Lien - a legal claim against property that must be satisfied when the property is sold.

Loan - money borrowed that is usually repaid with interest.

Loan Fraud - purposely giving incorrect information on a loan application in order to better qualify for a loan; may result in civil liability or criminal penalties.

Loan-to-Value (LTV) Ratio - a percentage calculated by dividing the amount borrowed by the price or appraised value of the home to be purchased. The higher the LTV, the less cash a borrower is required to pay as down payment.

Lock-in - since interest rates can change frequently, many lenders offer an interest rate lock-in that guarantees a specific interest rate if the loan is closed within a specific time.

Loss Mitigation - a process to avoid foreclosure. The lender tries to help a borrower who has been unable to make loan payments and is in danger of defaulting on his or her loan

Margin - an amount the lender adds to an index to determine the interest rate on an adjustable rate mortgage.

Mortgage banker - a company that originates and resells them to secondary mortgage lenders like Fannie Mae or Freddie Mac.

Mortgage broker - a firm that originates and processes loans for a number of lenders.

Mortgage - a lien on the property that secures the promise to repay a loan.

Mortgage insurance - a policy that protects lenders against some or most of the losses that can occur when a borrower defaults on a mortgage loan. Mortgage insurance is required primarily for borrowers with a down payment of less than 20 percent of the home's purchase price.

Mortgage Insurance Premium (MIP) - a monthly payment that is usually part of the mortgage payment, paid by a borrower for mortgage insurance.

Mortgage Modification - a loss-mitigation option that allows a borrower to refinance and/or extend the term of the mortgage loan and thus reduce the monthly payments.

Offer - indication by a potential buyer of a willingness to purchase a home at a specific price; generally put forth in writing.

Origination fee - the charge for originating a loan, usually calculated in the form of points and paid at closing.

Origination - the process of preparing, submitting, and evaluating a loan application; generally includes a credit check, verification of employment, and a property appraisal.

Partial Claim - a loss-mitigation option offered by the FHA that allows a borrowers, with help from a lender, to get an interest-free loan from HUD to bring their mortgage payments up to date.

Principal, Interest, Taxes, and Insurance (PITI) - the four elements of a monthly mortgage payment. Payments of principal and interest go directly towards repaying the loan, while the portion that covers taxes and insurance (homeowner's and mortgage, if applicable) goes into an escrow account to cover the fees when they are due.

Private Mortgage Insurance (PMI) - privately-owned companies that offer standard and special affordable mortgage insurance programs for qualified borrowers with down payments of less than 20 percent of a purchase price.

Pre-approve - lender commits to lend to a potential borrower; commitment remains as long as the borrower still meets the qualification requirements at the time of purchase.

Pre-foreclosure sale - allows a defaulting borrower to sell the mortgaged property to satisfy the loan and avoid foreclosure.

Premium - an amount paid on a regular schedule by a policyholder that maintains insurance coverage.

Prepayment - payment of the mortgage loan before the scheduled due date; may be subject to a prepayment penalty.

Pre-qualify - a lender informally determines the maximum amount an individual is eligible to borrow.

Principal - the amount borrowed from a lender; doesn't include interest or additional fees.

Real estate agent - an individual who is licensed to negotiate and arrange real estate sales; works for a real estate broker.

Realtor - a real estate agent or broker who is a member of the NATIONAL ASSOCIATION OF REALTORS, and its local and state associations.

Refinancing - paying off one loan by obtaining another. Refinancing is generally done to secure better loan terms (like a lower interest rate).

Rehabilitation Mortgage - a mortgage that covers the costs of rehabilitating (repairing or improving) a property. Some rehabilitation mortgages - like the FHA's 203(k) - allow a borrower to roll the costs of rehabilitation and home purchase into one mortgage loan.

Real Estate Settlement Procedures Act (RESPA) - a law protecting consumers from abuses during the residential real estate purchase and loan process by requiring lenders to disclose all settlement costs, practices, and relationships

Settlement - another name for closing.

Special Forbearance - a loss-mitigation option where the lender arranges a revised repayment plan for the borrower that may include a temporary reduction or suspension of monthly loan payments.

Subordinate - to place in a rank of lesser importance or to make one claim secondary to another.

Survey - a property diagram that indicates legal boundaries, easements, encroachments, rights of way, improvement locations, etc.

Sweat equity - using labor to build or improve a property as part of the down payment

Title 1 - an FHA-insured loan that allows borrowers to make non-luxury improvements (like renovations or repairs) to their home. Title I loans less than $7,500 don't require a property lien.

Title insurance - insurance that protects the lender against any claims that arise from arguments about ownership of the property; also available for homebuyers.

Title search - a check of public records to be sure that the seller is the recognized owner of the real estate and that there are no unsettled liens or other claims against the property.

Truth-in-Lending Act - a federal law obligating a lender to give full written disclosure of all fees, terms, and conditions associated with the loan.

Underwriting - the process of analyzing a loan application to determine the amount of risk involved in making the loan. It includes a review of the potential borrower's credit history and a judgment of the property value.

VA - **Department of Veterans Affairs**: a federal agency which guarantees loans made to veterans. Similar to mortgage insurance, a loan guarantee protects lenders against loss that may result from a borrower default.

About the Author

John A. Palumbo is CEO and founder of the Sales DNA Institute, an idea studio and research laboratory for sales and marketing management. Since 1985, he has presented hundreds of dynamic, visionary speeches and seminars internationally on the science of sales and influence. John is a member of the National Speakers Association and brings humor and animation to the platform to help others exceed their sales goals.

John has been instrumental in restructuring the Sales DNA of thousands of individuals from small, family run companies to large scale developers such as Trump Grande International. He has the ability to take individuals and organizations to new dimensions of selling excellence. With more than three decades of selling experience, John has closed over one billion dollars in real estate sales.

He is recipient of The National Association of Home Builders' Sales Manager of the Year Award and The Million Dollar Circle Lifetime Award. He is a prominent member of the Institute of Residential Marketing and has been an instructor for the institute for more than 15 years.

John's other books include *Selling at the Bottom of the Market, Close and Grow Rich, What's Your Sales DNA?* and *Salesnosis: The Art of Hypnotic Persuasion.*

Selling at the Bottom of the Market
A Seven Minute Presentation

How would you like to have a private coaching session with one of the nation's leading sales experts? John's newest book is exactly that. The unique, graphic design takes you from start to finish of precisely what to say *and write* with your next prospective buyer to boost your ability to close more sales … in even the toughest markets. John has answered the question all sales professionals are asking: "How do we sell to prospects that are afraid of making a buying mistake?" Buyers exist in every market – learn John's simple revelations and ensure that they convert to your sale and not someone else's.

www.**SellingAtTheBottom**.com

Close and Grow Rich
Fourteen Untapped Powers You Already
Have to Close Your Next Deal

No scripts to memorize, no new strategies, no reinventing the wheel ... this book reveals the 14 closing skills you already have that just need reawakening and perfecting. After closing well over a billion dollars' worth of deals, John has learned that there is no one strategy for getting closed business – by his count, there are 14 immutable skills to mastering the art of closing.

www.**CloseAndGrowRich**.com

What's Your Sales DNA?
Discover the Hidden Forces that are
Stopping You from Making Millions

As a highly sought after judge for Professional Achievement
Awards for over 20 years, John has collected data from all over
the country and discovered what sets the *really good* sales agents
apart from the *truly great* Sales Masters. *What's Your Sales DNA?*
reveals the results of John's research and will cause you to take an
introspective look at the hidden forces that are holding you back
from making millions.

www.MySalesDNA.com

Salesnosis
The Art of Hypnotic Persuasion

If you are a salesperson, entrepreneur, or business owner set in old, traditional ways of selling, this book may not be for you. However, for the hungry and open-minded, *Salesnosis* offers a powerful and revolutionary approach to capturing a prospect's attention, building credibility, and achieving influence. Turn your next presentation into an irresistible offer with these cutting-edge techniques for any sales situation. Regardless of what you're selling, mastering the art of hypnotic persuasion will create a sudden increase in sales — and dramatically boost your bank account.

www.**Salesnosis**.com